Anne and Peter Thomas

The Children's Party Book

For birthdays and other occasions

Illustrated by Anjo Mutsaars

Floris Books

D0183725

Categories and Symbols

Age
As indicated in the text.

Number of players

4   Number of players

4⁺   Minimum number

*If number not specified, any
number can play.*

Type of activity

O   Circle game

♛   Team game

     Paper and pencil

♪   Game with music

◍   Ball game

▶   What you need

Where to play
*If not otherwise indicated,
games are suitable for both
indoors and outdoors.*

Translated by Polly Lawson
Design & photography by Ernst
Thomassen
Things to make by Petra Berger

First published in Dutch under the title
Kom je ook op mijn feestje?
by Christoffor Publishers, Zeist, in 1998

First published in English in 1998
by Floris Books
Second edition 2008

British Library CIP Data available

ISBN 978-086315-639-7

Printed in China

Contents

Foreword

There are various occasions for throwing parties for children. The most important of course is their birthday, but you can also throw a farewell party if you are going to move house, or a welcome home party if your child has been in hospital for a long time. Passing an exam can also be an occasion for a party.

This book is about parties for parents to arrange for their children. It is wonderful for a child to have a party held in their honour, and you will find it very satisfying if the party is a success.

Our starting point in this book is the age and developmental stage of the child. The ideas for games, making things and puppet shows are designed for three and four-year-olds to eleven and twelve-year-olds.

You may feel nervous about organizing a party all by yourself, especially as your child grows older and friends tend to take over and prescribe how the party should be! It is therefore good to start your own traditions right from the beginning, when your children are still very small, taking into account your own family situation and its limitations. Your children's parties will then have their own special character, and these parties will become something your child remembers and looks forward to, wondering what you have in store for them.

Tiny details can give the party its own special quality, for instance the food on the table, a loaf of home-baked bread in a special shape, home-made paper chains and other decorations and so on.

One father remembered how every year at the beginning of a party he would tell a new made-up story. The story contained elements which reappeared later in the games, or which children had to remember in the guessing-games.

In a single parent family it can be more challenging to establish a party routine, but you may have a friend or relation who is able to help with preparations and with the party itself.

In this book we have tried to outline as much as possible of what throwing parties for children entails. We have based this on the experience of parties with our own children. Many parents and other party givers have also helped us by sharing their experiences. We are extremely grateful to them all.

This book contains all the ingredients for a successful party:

- *over 240 games, arranged according to type*
- *a comprehensive index showing the age for which the game is suitable, whether it is indoor or outdoor, how many children it involves etc.*
- *an extensive chapter on puppet shows*

A puppet theatre and puppet shows are frequently mentioned throughout the book. Chapter 10 deals with these in more detail.

Indexes
At the end of the book there are two indexes: an alphabetical index of games and things to make, and another index of games by type of activity, subdivided by age.

Symbols
The symbols used are shown on page 2 and page 39.

Anne and Peter Thomas

1 Games at Different Ages

When considering which games to play it is important to consider what is appropriate for the ages of the children involved.

Up to three years old

During their first three years children develop from being helpless creatures to bright little characters. They are constantly watching to see what is going on around them. They take everything in and copy what they see. Every day they see something new which they imitate in their own way. They are always trailing after you, wanting to do everything you do: washing up, baking cakes, bathing their baby brother or sister, and so on.

Toddlers prattle away all day long, first in simple single words and later in whole sentences. They refer to themselves by their own names: for example, 'Tom wants to bake a cake too!'

Then one day your child surprises you by calling himself or herself 'I.' Something important has happened. Your child has discovered that he or she is a person too. For us this came when our child was in his third year and it was the time we gave our first simple party. We set up some puppets on a table and played a few simple games in a circle.

Over three years old

At this stage you will notice that children's play begins to change. They play with whatever they happen to see or whatever comes within their reach. Objects can easily change their identity, for example, at one moment a simple rag can be a doll, then a blanket and then, later, a pond.

From this stage onwards children play tirelessly. They can go on baking cakes endlessly in the sandpit. It does not matter if there are already huge numbers of cakes as long as they can go on creating new ones. As children grow older they become more prepared to let other children play with them. Their play becomes more social.

In his book *Phases of Childhood* Bernard Lievegoed (Floris Books, p.73) writes that 'the repetition of the creative process in a seemingly endless rhythm is typical of play during this period. The child can remember things in a rhythmical form for which it has no abstract memory.' This is why rhythm and repetition are something which occur over and over again in the games of children of this age.

Four and five years old

You will gradually notice children starting to outgrow the patterns of their early childhood. They begin to play differently, needing to see a purpose and a result rather than their play being an end in itself. They want to use real things; whereas before they might have used a box or piece of wood or anything they could lay their hands on to represent a car, now they want something that actually resembles a real car. Naturally this is a gradual process occurring differently with each child.

Six and seven years old

Children of this age are really enjoyable. They can occupy themselves enthusiastically with all sorts of things and they are great fun to have about the house. You can have proper conversations with children of this age, but you may also find that they are no longer so open towards adults as they were when they were learning from them by imitation. Their own inner world begins to develop, as does their awareness of everything around them. Increasingly they want to know why, and they are beginning to think independently.

Seven to nine years old

Parents with children between seven and nine are kept busy with their young ones eager to learn and wanting to know exactly how things work and what they are for, as their ability to think develops.

Usually children at this stage are sociable and friendly. There is still a strong natural bond with their parents, but it becomes necessary to explain clearly why you want something done in a certain way. At this stage of life children find it challenging and exciting to play games in which all kinds of mysteries have to be unravelled.

Ten years old

Almost all children go through a hard time around their tenth year. They may become quite difficult, perhaps being critical and rude. They suddenly find everything they used to do childish. They may develop new fears, for example, fear of the dark. The internal world of children of this age moves between extremes: one moment they are happy and carefree, the next moment they are deeply upset. They may vehemently criticize one character and hero-worship another.

These are the first early signs of adolescence, the period in which young people are searching for their own identity. They tend to congregate in cliques, usually of one sex, and are very conscious of who is 'in' or 'out.' This is obviously very significant in terms of who is to be invited to a party.

At this stage young people are increasingly conscious of their gender. Boys become aware of their own strength. Girls may develop strong ideas about the way things should be done and they often want to follow the current fashion.

Eleven and twelve years old

Fortunately in the following years the conflicting extremes of early adolescence gradually even out and children become more harmonious. However, a new situation may arise between adults and children of this age. An eleven or twelve-year-old may look straight at you, observing the person you really are and the ideals you stand for. This is when parents realize that the influence they have over their children is diminishing.

2 Parties at Different Ages

The following categories give a rough indication of the age suitability of each game.

Age category

Age 3–4

Age 5–6

Age 7–9

Age 10+

Most games in this book have a youngest age limit at which they can be played happily, but they can often be played successfully with older children. For example, you can play *Musical chairs* with pre-school children but seven to nine-year-olds will also enjoy it.

Parties may vary enormously but it is always a good idea to maintain a balance between action games and quieter activities which require the children to be observant or creative.

There are indications whether the game is to be played indoors or outside, how many players are required, whether it is a group game, a game played in a circle, a team game and so on. You will find a key to these symbols on page 2 and on page 39 (at the beginning of Chapter 9).

Three and four years old

Little children need to have everything acted out in front of them as they rely entirely on imitation. They are not yet ready to take turns and do not really play with one another.

It's therefore better not to let the party go on for too long (one hour at the most) and to limit the numbers to a few children. Remember that two of the possible activities suggested may fill the hour, so don't be too ambitious or plan too much.

Possible activities:
- singing, clapping and finger games
- painting (with watercolours)
- decorating cakes
- a puppet-show

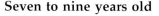

Possible activities:
- circle games
- word games and riddles
- relay races
- hiding, ball games and catch
- puppet show, for instance as an introduction to an outside game or a treasure hunt
- simple group games
- a simple treasure hunt
- baking bread figures or cookies
- potato printing

Five and six years old

Young children can manage all sorts of games with the help of an adult. A party for this age group can last for two to two and a half hours.

Children's love of repetition can be given full rein in songs and games played in a circle. Children of this age are usually too young to take part in competitive games. They may enjoy making something together which they can take home. You can also do a puppet show with a simple story, or a traditional, exciting Punch and Judy show.

Possible activities:
- action songs and games
- circle games
- simple games such as hide and seek, ball games, simple relays
- decorating cakes or baking cookies
- crafts: folding paper and stickers
- reading or telling stories
- a puppet show

Seven to nine years old

You can demand quite a bit more of children of this age and they should be ready for games with rules. The games can now become more complicated, challenging the enormous energy which children have and giving them the opportunity to show what they can do. Children of this age enjoy a certain amount of competition, so team games and relay races may be popular. There are also plenty of guessing games and games involving calculations. Of course the best team gets a prize, but take care, as seven and eight-year-olds cannot always cope with losing. You can avoid problems by giving the real winners a prize for their skill, another team a prize for ingenuity and a booby prize for the losing team. Children feel that it is important to win something which they can take home with them (see also page 12).

Over ten years old

From about the age of ten onwards children want to celebrate their birthdays quite differently from before. At this age they have become critical and are concerned that their parties should not be too babyish. Games with a competitive element are the trend, as are games in which they can show their skills.

Possible activities:
- word games and riddles
- relay races
- more extensive scouting games
- complicated treasure hunts

3 Parents' Questions

When should we hold a party?

If possible it is nice if the party can be on the afternoon of the child's real birthday so that it forms part of the birthday celebrations. Older schoolchildren who are coming without their parents can be invited on a free afternoon after school. The parents can then collect their children at an agreed time after the party.

Some parents wish to keep the actual birthday of the child as something special rather than letting it become swamped by a party and all that that entails. In that case the party can take place on another afternoon. You can discuss dates beforehand with the parents of the other children. This will avoid disappointments. Remember that children of separated parents may be with the other parent at the weekend.

How many children should we invite?

A rule of thumb is to invite as many children as the age of your own child, and in practice this usually works very well. But think of yourself, too. Don't invite more children than you can cope with. Consider the space available. If your house is small you may prefer not to have too many children at the party.

The character of the birthday child is also an important factor. Some children are quiet and introverted. They tend to sit in a corner in a crowd and not say anything. They have few friends and hardly play with other children. Such children may really enjoy having one friend to play for the afternoon, perhaps staying for supper. These type of children may want you to play with them too. This prevents the birthday child withdrawing halfway through the afternoon and the other child (or children) going and playing by themselves.

At the other extreme is the child who is everybody's friend and wants to invite everyone to their birthday party. However, even with older children who are able to talk about what they are going to do, it is probably better to limit the numbers to a maximum of twelve.

If you are going to play games with children aged between five and seven, four to six children should be plenty.

If games are going to be an important part of the party you may need a minimum number of players. Some group games can be played with three or four children but most games can only be played properly if you have five or more participants. If the games are competitive you will probably need two teams, in which case you will need a minimum of six or even eight children.

Always make sure that you have enough help. If you are going out with the children have someone with you in case of emergency.

Who should we invite?

Sometimes it is difficult to decide who your child can and cannot invite. You may wonder whether or not to invite the neighbour's children even though they may not know your child's school friends. And then there is the question of whether to invite everyone in the child's class at school.

These sorts of questions usually crop up at about the age of seven, once the children have established their own friends. Up to that time you usually know which children your child plays with and which ones they would like to invite. Children between nine and twelve generally know who they want to invite to their party. You may have to put the brakes on a bit for they may want to invite half the world, so discuss with them how many children it will be practical to have at the party.

It is often fine to invite both the children from the neighbourhood as well as your child's school friends. The children will be so busy playing games, eating cakes, watching the puppet show, listening to the story, and so on, that they won't have time to stop and notice that they don't know everyone very well.

As the children grow older the question of exactly who is invited becomes more and more important. This is the age when children make their own circle of friends and it may be difficult to invite one child and not another. If the children are going to play group and team games you can invite a larger group if you have plenty of room. However, this may be daunting for any children who don't know many of the others and they might feel a bit lost. It might be better to do something different with those children at another time.

See what your child's class is like socially and how your child fits in. Sometimes it is important for your child not only to invite their friends but also anyone with whom they have problems. The party then becomes an opportunity to make a break-through. You may also want to discuss this beforehand with the child's teacher.

Should little brothers and sisters be at the party too?

The activities of the party must be appropriate for the age of the birthday child. You can then consider whether they are suitable for younger brothers and sisters. If the age differences of the children in the family are not too great it is good if brothers and sisters can be there too, for they do belong. One of them might be able to be an assistant team leader. But sometimes younger children can be a disturbance at a party for older children as they may be too young to take part and become a bit resentful. It is difficult to solve this kind of problem during the party. Consider beforehand how the little brothers and sisters will behave during the party. It might be better for them to go to a friend's house, or to invite one of their own friends to the party.

How long should a party last?

This depends on the age of the children, the numbers involved and the activities planned. The following examples give an indication.

Age four
The birthday child has just turned four and the children are coming to the party in the afternoon. The children arrive, presents are given, games are played and the birthday cake enjoyed. In total, it should last one to one and a half hours.

Age six
Your child has turned six. You have organized a party and invited six children. The children arrive and

presents are given. They then play with toys or have a puppet show, play games and then have tea and birthday cake. This will easily take one and a half to two and a half hours.

Age seven to nine
A party for children of this age will need a proper plan. A treasure-hunt or similar activity would take about one hour, so the whole party might last two to three hours.

Age ten and over
If older children have not opted for an outing you will have to offer them a series of activities with games and tasks which will demand their full attention. Children of this age also like sitting together chatting and eating party food. Depending on the number of activities the party can last a whole afternoon.

The duration of a party

Age 3-4	1–1½ hours
Age 5-6	1½–2½ hours
Age 7-9	2–3 hours
Age 7-9	3–4 hours

Should the winner get a prize?

Prizes are given when someone does something more quickly, better or perhaps more gracefully than someone else. This competitive element is important only after age six or seven, as little children respond better to group games.

You can always 'help' to make sure no-one is disadvantaged in competitive games. For example, in the game *Pick the raisin* (p.42) one child goes out of the room. There are lots of raisins on the table and the remaining children choose one of them. The child comes in again and picks up one raisin after another. As soon as they pick the right raisin everyone cries 'Stop!' The child has to put back that raisin but they keep the ones they have already taken. Then the next child has a turn. If they take the right raisin straight away, and so don't get the chance to keep any, you can slip them a few extra ones.

For children aged eight and nine it is important that everyone gets something. Children below this age often can't cope with losing, but a party is not really the right occasion for teaching them. If you are having a relay race with two or more teams make sure that you have enough prizes, so that every team and perhaps even every child gets a prize. With a little imagination you can invent a reason why each group completing a task should get a prize. For example, you could tell one team that they were the fastest, another that they were the most original, and another that they produced the most beautiful result.

Some games highlight the achievement of an individual, and in many cases the reward comes naturally as part of the game, like being 'it' when playing catch.

Should we give out a present list for our child?

You may be amazed at the expensive presents given at some parties and wonder whether they really give the recipient pleasure.

It is better to stick to modest presents at children's parties. A list of requests may ensure that this is the case. For little children, make up the list yourself. Children of over six or seven can do it with you. This will help prevent the child being given presents of which you do not really approve. You can enclose the present list with the invitation, although some parents may consider that to be presumptuous. It might therefore be better to discuss the choice of presents with the other parents, if you feel you can.

4 The Birthday

Amid all the hustle and bustle of everyday family life it is easy to get bogged down in the practicalities of what will happen on your child's birthday. It can be a good idea to stop and think about the birthday in another way. After all it is your child's *anniversary*. One year has been completed and another one is about to begin, so it is good to reflect on this and how things are changing. So much happens in the lives of young children that it can help to think back on the past year, for yourself as well as for them.

On a child's first birthday you look back on the development of a tiny creature, lying almost passively, into a child that boldly crawls about the room, always ready to express their needs. There may have been worrying times. On the eve of the birthday, look at the photo album and reflect on the pictures of the past year or talk about them with your partner. In this way you will conclude the year for your child and for yourself. Some mothers write about the pictures which are the most significant for them and re-read what they have written at the end of the following year.

There may have been difficulties, illnesses or character problems for your child, but there will also have been external influences. Just before their birthday you can look at all these things more objectively and see them in perspective as part of the development of your child.

Once children have reached the age of about four you can include them in your reminiscences. Let the birthday begin on the evening before when you are putting them to bed by talking about the events of the past year. Children love this.

When they are a bit older they can take an active part in the conversation, and you can also talk about the following day, the birthday itself.

There are all sorts of ways of making a birthday special for children. When you ask children later what they remember of their birthdays, they will often talk about how they did not have to lay the table or do chores and could choose what they wanted to eat. They will also remember how wonderful it was to be the centre of attention on that day.

In our home, the birthday child wakes up and knows at once 'It's my birthday!' They get washed and get dressed as usual but have to wait until they are allowed to come down. The rest of the family have decked out the festive breakfast-table, and a decorated chair stands ready for the birthday child. Then everyone begins to sing and they know that they may come down. This was when presents were given in our family. The rest of the day is spent differently each year. Often other members of the family and friends come round to wish the child a happy birthday, and perhaps in the afternoon there is a party.

Once the special day is over you will probably be worn out, but first you will have to tidy up. Sometimes by this stage parents might think that the party is over and it's time to get back to real life, but is this really the case for the child?

Some children will want to play with their presents right away, while others want to sit quietly in a corner and savour the memory of it all. Usually the birthday child wants to talk about everything they have experienced during the day.

Looking back over the day at bedtime gives the child a chance to digest all the experiences and store them as a special memory.

It might be nice if a friend is allowed to stay the night after the party, and they can look at the presents together. Before the child goes to sleep you or your partner can talk over the birthday with them, and if another child is staying the night they can join in the conversation, too. Sometimes, especially for younger children, it is nice if the day after their birthday, the first day of their new age, can be spent exclusively with their parents, marking it as a special milestone for children and parents alike.

5 Preparing for a Party

Parents who are experienced party givers will have an established routine. This chapter may be useful for those new to party giving.

When preparing for the party you will need to consider:

- *the games and activities the children will be doing*
- *the invitations*
- *the decorations*
- *the food and drink*
- *the wishes of the child*
- *presents for children who are coming*

Once you have decided on what will happen at the party you can do the invitations. The type of activities you choose will depend on the number of children you are going to invite and their age, and whether or not you are going to give the party a theme. Opposite is a checklist to help you in the preparatory stages. You can adapt the list to suit your circumstances.

Beginning the preparations

It will take longer to prepare for the first party you give than for any subsequent ones. One mother told us that she was preoccupied with her child and his birthday for weeks before the event. As ideas came to her she wrote them down in a notebook, gradually accumulating all sorts of possibilities.

If your party is going to involve the sort of activities which your child does regularly you only need to start the preparations a week or two beforehand. Send out the invitations two or three weeks before the party. At this stage, you will need to know what is going to happen at the party although you do not need to have worked out all the details.

If you have decided to tell a story, give a puppet show with home-made puppets or play slightly more difficult games, you will need more time for the preparations. Depending on how much time you have available you will need to begin two or three weeks in advance, in order to make paper chains, bake bread and plan the games. If the children are going to help, you should not start too early but you will need to cater for the fact that it takes longer when they are involved. The following calendar may be of help during your preparations.

Calendar

6–4 weeks before:
- prepare the puppet show and/or story
- make the puppets

3 weeks before:
- see what your child is most enjoying doing
- plan party activities accordingly

3–2 weeks before:
- prepare the invitations

2 weeks before:
- make preparations with the birthday child
- send out the invitations

2–1 weeks before:
- make the decorations
- try out the treasure hunt

1 week before:
- for a party for little ones: invite one or two parents with their children
- make the decorations
- go shopping

The day before:
- last minute preparations
- bake the cake
- hang up the paper chains
- organize the room

Checklist

When is the party?
Date, start and finishing time

Who is invited?
Name, address and telephone
number of each child

Write out a present list (optional)

Helpers
Helpers during the party
Babysitters for younger ones

Inside or outside?
Decide on place
If outside, will it be in a garden, a
park, a playground or woods?
Weather forecast
Type of clothing recommended
(warm clothes or rainwear?)

Parties with a theme
Find a story
Prepare a puppet show
Organize clothes for dressing up
Props

Invitations
Cards and envelopes
Stamps

Setting up
Have ready coat-hangers with the
names of the children coming
Prepare the rooms
Set up a table for the presents

Decorations
Materials
Hang up paper chains
Decorate the table
Decorate the birthday child's table
and chair
Find party clothes and party hats

Presents and prizes
Make or buy them
Prepare baskets and bags for the
presents

The meal
Lay the table
Place-cards for all the children
Decide on the food
Write a shopping list
Have ready a festive table cloth or
place mats, plates and cups
Check there is enough cutlery
Bake and decorate a birthday cake
Make or buy lemonade and buy
drinking straws

Preparing for the activities
Get the materials and tools (e.g.
scissors, pencils, paints and glue)
Have paper or newspaper ready to
protect the table

Games
Write a list of possibilities
List materials needed for each game
and have them ready
Prepare a game to get to know each
other at the beginning
Prepare a short stand-by game to
fill a gap or use up extra time

Treasure hunt
Decide on the route and the
treasure!
Set up the treasure hunt

Organizing transport
(if necessary)

Shopping list

15

The child's wishes

Children age 3-4 do not usually have any specific wishes for their parties but they are very interested in what the adults are doing and they will enjoy decorating the invitations.

Children around six years old may know exactly what they want to do at their party. Where possible you can go along with their wishes and involve them as much as possible in the preparations. They can help make the invitations, prepare the meal and bake the cake.

If older children have special wishes for their birthday party they can help make them happen as well as helping with the general preparations. Children over nine and ten sometimes have very precise ideas about what they want. They too can help with the preparations.

Naturally your child will be the centre of attention during the party, so they can be a bit spoilt and need not work too hard. It's a good idea to prevent the birthday child from helping too much as they may become one of the organizers rather than playing with friends.

We always tried to keep one aspect of our children's parties a surprise even for them; for example, the puppet show or the treasure hunt. It is particularly exciting to keep aspects of theme parties a surprise.

The invitations

Children will often talk to their friends about their party for a long time before the date and they may already have invited them. There may have already been contact with the parents of the various children. But the proper written invitations must always be sent out at least two weeks before the party. If you give the invitations to children under seven by hand you run the risk of the invitations not reaching their destination. Parents have occasionally discovered a heap of invitations in their child's pocket a day or two before the party. It is therefore better to send the invitations by post or to give them to the child in the presence of an adult.

Include any details about, for example, special clothes for a party with a theme, or anything else required, such as swimming costumes, with the invitation.

Clearing the room

If possible it is good to take all surplus furniture out of the room where the party is to be held, so that there is plenty of room. Remove anything that might be spoiled or damaged, or that is particularly precious, and put it in a safe place. Toys or other objects which are easily broken or which the birthday child does not want others to play with should be put away carefully.

Prizes and little presents

Game prizes and presents which the children can take home with them can be laid out beforehand, perhaps in a festive basket or box. You may prefer to let the children make something which they can take home with them (see Chapter 9). This can be a sociable and constructive part of the party. Make sure that the children take their presents home with them at the end of the party. You can give each child a bag for the presents and anything they have made, plus any prizes they win.

When buying prizes make sure they are all roughly the same size.

Children will soon notice if someone else has got something bigger. If the children are making the prizes themselves during the party it will not matter so much if they are not exactly the same size.

If the children are going to bake bread rolls, prepare a few extra ones so that you can give them to anyone whose roll does not rise properly.

Prizes and presents you can buy:
- a bag of nuts, raisins, little cookies or sweets (candy)
- a pot with bulbs (in early spring)
- a little polished stone
- a candle (in winter)
- a photo of the party if you are able to print quickly from a digital camera
- a packet of origami paper

- a pencil or a little packet of coloured crayons
- little cake tins
- a whistle
- marbles
- a drawing pad
- a few small tubes of paint and a paint brush
- balls of wool
- a packet of seeds
- a bubble blowing set
- a small set of face paints
- a frisbee
- beeswax or plasticine

Prizes and presents which you can make yourself:
- paper flowers (see p.30)
- a little note pad
- a festive crown (see p.27)
- a whirligig (see p.64)
- a felt gnome (see p.32)
- a home-made candle (see p.32)
- a woollen doll (see p.33)
- a window transparency (see p.33)
- a decorated box with a little stone or crystal in it

Presents which you can make with your children:
- a bread figure (see p.63)
- a decorated cake (see p.62)
- a window transparency (see p.33)
- a home-made candle (see p.32)
- a festive crown (see p.27)
- a whirligig (see p.64)
- a T-shirt with a picture (see p.66)

17

6 Parties with a Theme

A theme gives a party some defined content, and a theme which reflects a child's enthusiasms and interests will give great pleasure. Begin the party with a story or a puppet show in order to introduce the theme (see *Telling a story,* p.38 and *Puppet shows and Puppet theatre,* Chapter 10, p.94).

The theme can run through everything you do during the party. In the *Doll family party* the children eat little dolls' cakes from a toy tea-set and the games are short and simple. If the theme is a fairy tale this will affect everything that happens. In the tale of *The apple cake* the children obviously eat apple cake and apples appear in all kinds of games. You can change the name of games or parts of games to fit with the theme, though the rest of the games do not need to be changed.

The giants' party is a good example of a party with a theme. Suggestions for the content of other party-themes are also given.

How to find a story
You can look for an appropriate story in collections of fairy tales in the local library. Use the list of library books or ask the librarian for help if necessary. If the story is too long you can summarize it. Adapt it to fit your situation, especially if you are going to act it out with the children afterwards.

Dressing up clothes
Theme parties naturally need clothes for dressing up. You can write suggestions for costumes on the invitations, but be prepared and have some costumes spare. Some children may feel that they do not fit in, or may not find appropriate costumes at home.

If you prefer to have complete control of the costumes you will have to make them yourself. The children do not need to be completely disguised: a hat and a tie, a coat or a scarf may be all that is necessary. The children can put on the fancy-dress clothes when they arrive.

The games and activities mentioned below are described in Chapter 9, and can be found in the index.

The giants' party
Age 5–9

Invitation:
A picture of a big giant, sticking up above the top of the main part of the card, or a picture of a big chest with a lock on it.

There are lots of stories about giants in folk tales.

Giants are huge and clumsy and their belongings are all enormous. Many stories tell us how strong giants are, but they are also very silly! They are not as clever as people so they steal the things they can't make or find for themselves. Nevertheless, you need to be very cunning to get the better of giants.

- The children arrive, hang up their coats and go and sit down (see p.35).
- The presents are given out and unwrapped (see p.35).
- Now it is time for the story. In stories about giants there is usually a cunning hero who outwits the giant in the end. If you are telling the story as a puppet show you can put on a special scary voice for the giant. You may only need two puppets, the giant and a child.

The giant appears and says that he is looking for something to eat and something to play with. But people are so small that the things in their houses are much too small for him.

'Now you all know that I am a strong giant. No one is as strong as I am. I don't have to work. I can get everything I want from people.'

Then a child arrives. 'Good morning, giant. You're very big! What did you say? Can you get everything you want?'

'Yes, I am so strong that everyone is afraid of me, I can just take everything I want - people just don't dare come and get it back.'

And then the giant says that he has just found all sorts of delicious things in someone's house. He has put everything in a box and taken it away: cake, lemonade, ice-cream.

- At this point you say, 'Hey, wait a moment, that sounds like all the delicious things we've got for tea. Come and see if everything is still there. Oh no! It's all gone!'

  So the children have to go and look for the giant (birthday child's father or adult friend). Somewhere in the house or garden they find the giant, but he has fallen fast asleep.

- Explain that because you are big too, you know a lot about giants. Tell the children that they will have to think up a spell to wake him up.
- The giant is woken by the children's spell and now they can ask him questions to find out where all the birthday goodies have gone. Very quickly they realize that the giant is so sleepy that he can answer only 'yes' and 'no.'
- Eventually the children get enough information from the giant to be able to find the box. They find that it is padlocked, and so they have to go back to the giant to find out how they can open it. Once again the giant answers only 'yes,' 'no,' or 'perhaps.' He lets the children go on asking questions until they ask him for a clue. Then he gives them a piece of paper showing part of a puzzle and tells them where they can find the next bit of the puzzle. When the children have found all the pieces of the puzzle they put them together and read where the key is. In the end they find the well-earned cake and eat it.

Possible indoor activities:
Hot or cold, p.50; All birds can fly, p.54; I'm going on a journey, p.55; Fizz buzz, p.55; Who am I? p.41; Teapot, p.57; Paying forfeits, p.49; Blindfold games, p.70

Possible outoor activities:
Winkie, p.53; Passing the ring, p.53; Poor kitty, p.53; Grandmother's footsteps, p.75; Ferryman, may I cross? p.76; Catch across the circle, p.78; Sitting ball, p.79; Stand still, p.78

Doll family party
Age 5–6

Invitation:
Picture of a doll

This is an indoor party for boys as well as girls. Each child brings their favourite doll or animal.

- Before the party begins place some stools or low chairs in a circle. The children can also sit in a circle on the floor.
- When everyone is sitting say 'It's Annabel's birthday today and she's giving a party with her doll Lisa. Look, this is Lisa.'
- Go round the circle and help each child to say something about their doll, its name, how long they have had it and anything else that they want to say. Little children may need quite a bit of prompting, but older ones will have lots to say.
- When all the children have intro-duced their dolls they can take them with them as they give the birthday child a present.
- Now it's time for the story. Tell a short story, for example, the folk tale *Any Room for Me?* (also called *The Mitten*).

One day in winter an old man is walking through the forest with his dog when he loses his mitten. A little mouse sees the warm mitten and creeps into it. Then a frog comes by and wants to jump in too. Then a little hare arrives, followed by a fox, a wild boar and finally a bear. Each one says 'Can I come in too?' as they climb into the mitten. When the old man notices that he has lost his mitten his dog runs back and chases all the animals away.

- When you have finished telling the story say 'Let's go and act the story. The dolls can watch.'
- Make sure you have the following props ready: a big cloth for the mitten plus a headband for each child. The headbands show the pictures of the animals the children will act. (see *Crowns or headbands*, p.27).
- Tell the story again, but do it slowly and include long pauses so that each animal has a chance to climb into the 'mitten.' Prompt the children softly so that they can each repeat their lines.

If the children want to you can repeat the performance, though you might have to leave out another game if you are running short of time.

- After the performance the dolls will be tired and will need to be put to bed. Each child lays down their doll and covers it with a little cloth or blanket.
- At this point games for the dolls' mothers and fathers can begin.
- Finish the games in time so that the dolls can be got out of bed.
- The party ends with lemonade and tiny doll cakes.

Possible indoor activities:
Painting, p.63; Decorating cakes, p.62; Baking bread figures (for the dolls), p.63; Circle games, p.51; Pick the raisin, p.42; Biting the cake, p.47; Pin tail on donkey, p.70.
Possible indoor activities:
Action songs and games, p.43; Circle games, p.51.

The apple cake
Age 5–6

Invitation:
Picture of a large apple

An old woman really wants to eat an apple cake, but she has no apples, only plums. She goes and exchanges the plums for feathers, the feathers for flowers, the flowers for a chain, the chain for a dog, and the dog for apples.

You can create a whole party round

- Before the party make two identical sets of cards. Keep one set back and put the other in a basket. Each card shows a stage in the life of an apple: the apple tree laden with ripe apples, a branch with apple blossom, bees, an apple, apples being picked, a market stall with apples, an apple.
- Each child takes a card from the basket as they arrive and then they go and sit in a circle. The birthday child has the other set of cards, takes one out and asks who has the same card. The child with that card then gives their present.
- After that you can tell a story or give a puppet show. Ask the children questions as the story unfolds so that you bring them into it. You can act out the story as in the *Doll family party* or you can leave it as a puppet show. The characters do not all need to appear on stage as you can explain some of what happens.
- As apples are autumn fruit, you can bring autumn and harvest into some of the later activities.

  The children can make a picture of an apple by sticking small pieces of coloured paper onto a backing sheet, or they can make a little transparency for a table or window (see p.33). You can also bake apple tarts or apple cakes with the children for them to take home.

Possible activities:
Bobbing for apples, p.74; *Kim's tasting game*, p.59; *Pick the raisin*, p.42; *Paying forfeits*, p.49; *Quiet circle games*, p.51.

Three Kings' festival

Invitation:
Picture of the Three Kings or a crown

The festival of the Three Kings comes in the middle of winter on January 6. The Three Kings saw in the stars that a new king had been born and they set off to bring him gifts. Even now in many parts of the world the journey of the Three Kings is re-enacted, sometimes with children singing as they pass the houses in their neighbourhood. In this version the kings wear red, blue and green cloaks. Bake a Three Kings loaf by putting three beans in the dough or cake mixture. Whoever finds a bean can be one of the Three Kings. The other children are Mary and Joseph and servants for the kings.

If your child's birthday is in January you can make their party a Three Kings' festival. Make sure that you have enough coloured sheets or costumes for dressing up.
- The children arrive, go and sit down and give out their presents (see p.35).
- The Three Kings' loaf is cut. The slices must be left standing otherwise the children might see which slices contain beans. As you go round with the loaf each

child takes a slice. The children must eat very carefully so as not to swallow any of the beans. If the beans are not all found the remaining kings can be chosen.

- Make the crowns and other remaining parts of the costumes with the children (see p.27). Then everyone dresses up.
- There are various stories about the journey of the Three Kings. While you are telling the story the children can draw pictures.
- After that it is time for games and the cake.

Variation:
Instead of acting a play you can make the Journey of the Three Kings the starting point for a treasure hunt. The kings and their servants each have to go on a long journey through all kinds of challenges. These challenges become the tasks of the treasure hunt. The children who have found the beans are the leaders of the group. The groups can be formed using *Numbering-off games* (see p.39).

Possible activities:
Forfeits, p.49; *Circle games,* p.51; *Memory, observation, word and guessing games,* p.54.

Witches' festival
Age 7–9 indoors

Invitation:
Picture of a witch on a broomstick, or a witch in a cottage

Witches look strange. They carry out their work in the half light and they are often spiteful. They never have enough and they put a spell on everything they can lay their hands on. People often get taken prisoner by witches or have to carry out various tasks. In Russian fairy tales there is a witch called Baba-Yaga. She will let you go if you can answer her questions.

You can take advantage of witches' tendency to ask questions during the party.

- The party begins with receiving and unwrapping the presents (see p.35)
- If possible you can transform one room into a witch's cottage. Keep it in semi-darkness and hang lamps or Chinese lanterns in it. The children go into the room and find a witch. The witch tells them who she is and where she comes from. She talks about herself. (You might want to use Baba-Yaga for this). The witch tells the children that they must carry out a series of tasks or else they will remain under her spell.
- The witch gives the children a list of tasks or questions (see *Quiz* p.58). Older children will respond to something quite challenging, for example a treasure hunt (see p.89). Once the task is completed the witch lets the children go and it is time for games and birthday cake and perhaps also a witches' dance.

Possible indoor activities:
Kim's game, p.59; *Guessing games,* p.51; *Witch's show (as a variation on a Fashion show),* p.61; *Charades,* p.61; *Potato printing,* p.66.
Possible outdoor activities:
Catch, p.75; *Witch's footsteps (a variation of Grandmother's footsteps)* p.75; *Witch, may I cross?* (variation) p.76; *Tree dens,* p.75; *Blindfold games,* p.70; *Relays with tasks,* p.84.

Summer festival
Age 5–10+ outdoors

Invitation:
Picture of a fire, a glass of lemonade with a straw, children playing in the sun.

As long as the weather is fine it's best to hold a summer party out of doors. You can play all sorts of games. A summer party does not require much preparation. A barbecue, baking bread (by putting pieces of dough on the end of sticks and baking them over a fire), and a camp fire all work well at a summer party. A camp fire naturally gives rise to story telling.

Possible activities:
Age 5–6: Ball games, p.78; *Catch,* p.75; *Relay races,* p.83 Age 7+: *Scouting games,* p.86

Quiet games:
Bobbing for apples, p.74; *Hoop-la,* p.74; *Knocking down the pyramid,* p.74; *Baton relays,* p.80

For hot weather:
Games with water, for instance *Firemen,* p.84

Dragon festival
Age 5–9

Invitation:
Picture of a dragon

There are various stories about dragons which you can use as the basis for a dragon theme party — look in the local library. Well-known stories in which the dragon is overcome are *St George and the Dragon* and *Michael and the Dragon*.

The theme of dragons is particularly suited to autumn. Dragons try to destroy life and the harvest and must therefore be conquered.

Begin the party indoors and if possible move outside later. Once the presents have been given the children could fly kites or go on a treasure hunt to find the dragon.

Kites
It's great fun to fly kites when the wind is blowing. Older children can make their own kites. You will need to be well prepared and make sure that you have the necessary materials in the house. It takes 30 to 40 minutes to make a very simple kite (see p.67). Younger children can make a whirligig (see p.64).

Treasure hunt
Do this outside if possible, though if the weather is bad you could do it indoors (see *Treasure Hunts* p.89). The dragon has to be tracked down; usually he is lying asleep in his den. The children follow the dragon's footprints. They have to creep along very cautiously and quietly so as not to wake him. As they follow the treasure hunt they have to find or make charms or devise other ways to overcome the dragon. Make sure the tasks for the treasure hunt are appropriate to the age of the children. For example, younger children might be asked to find something typical of harvest or autumn, such as chestnuts, acorns and coloured leaves. When they lay these things in a circle round the dragon the dragon's power disappears.

Possible indoor activities:
Simple group games, p.47; *Circle games*, p.51; *Memory and observation games*, p.54
Possible outdoor activities:
Ball games, p.78; *Games of skill*, p.74; *Relay races*, p.80; *Simple group games*, p.47.

Noah's ark

Age 7–9

Invitation:

Picture of a Noah's ark with one or more animals.

Noah and his three sons built a great ark in which a male and a female of every kind of animal could live while the earth was flooded and the ark floated upon the waters.

This Bible story offers endless possibilities for making things.

- After the presents have been unwrapped sit down with the children and tell the story of Noah's ark.
- The children can then make the ark and the animals using all kinds of materials. Use cardboard from cardboard boxes for the ark. Stick the various parts together with glue or sticky tape. When the ark is finished the children can paint it. It does not need to be a perfect model of a boat as long as the children enjoy making it.

- The animals can also be made from cardboard, or you can make them from quick-drying clay.
- When the ark is finished tell the children that Noah and his sons have to keep the animals busy during the voyage by playing games with them.
- Have ready some home-made cards with pictures of animals. You will need as many cards as there are children and there must be two cards for each animal. When the children need to form teams for playing games ask each child to pick a card. There will then be two teams, each with one version of each animal.
- At the end of the party the ark comes to rest on dry land and the animals come out into the world again. The children can take home the animals they have made.

Possible activities:

All birds can fly, p.54; *Pin the tail on the donkey*, p.70; *Cat and mouse*, p.53; *Poor kitty*, p.53; *Animal kim* (make up a variation), p.59; *Relay races* (you can make these in keeping with the theme by asking the children to creep like caterpillars, jump like frogs or hop like kangaroos with a cushion in front), p. 80; *Horse shoes*, p.86; *Horse and rider*, p.83

Music festival
Age 10+

Invitation:
Picture of a musical instrument or a pop-star.

If you have a group of musical and creative children music can provide a natural theme for the party. Possibilities:
- Hold a quiz with questions about composers, pop-groups and songs (see *Quiz* p.58).
- Let the children listen to various pieces of music and ask who composed the music or the song.
- Blindfold the children and ask them to guess the instrument.
- Ask the children to compose words for a well-known song in teams.

Possible activities:
Action songs and games, p.43; *Guessing games*, p.54; *Blindfold games*, p.70; *Baton relays*, p.83

Fashion show
Age 10+

Invitation:
Picture of a mannequin or a model on a catwalk

This party can be for boys as well as girls.
- The children are divided into groups and are given the task of making an elaborate hat or item of clothing.
- The clothes can be made from various kinds of paper or old bits of cloth. They can be sewn or fastened together or stuck together with sticky tape.
- Accessories and jewellery can be made from thin wire, beads, bits of wood, corks, coloured paper, peanuts, pasta shapes and so on.
- Applying make-up to each other can be a separate part of the party.
- Once the clothes and accessories are ready the fashion show can begin. Each child can parade their own creation. It will be especially fun if the type of music used at fashion shows can be played. If possible give the participants a photo of their creation to take home with them.

Possible activities:
The children will be fully occupied for most of the party, but if necessary some action games will provide some variety, for instance: *Winkie*, p.53; *Musical chairs*, p.69; *Team tug*, p.77; *Ring the bell*, p.71; *Dress on six*, p.72; *Spin the plate*, p.75; *Three way pull*, p.75; *Over the line*, p.77; *Apples and pears*, p.77.

7 Invitations, Hats, Paper Chains and Presents

Invitations

▶ *Cards and envelopes, a knife,*
coloured pencils and/or paints,
materials to make a collage, balloons.
If the numbers are small enough
you can handwrite the invitations,
which give a more personal feel.
Otherwise they can be photocopied.
You can decorate the invitation in
lots of different ways. Children over
about five can help with this.

Put the following information on
an invitation:
- *the reason for the party*
- *the address*
- *the date, time and duration of party*
- *RSVP*
- *any special instructions*
- *suggestions for presents (if desired)*
- *you could also include a line*
  requesting parents to let you know if
  there is any particular food their
  child should not be given

Remember to:
- *check beforehand whether the*
  invitations fit the envelopes
- *write the name of the child on the*
  envelope before inserting the card
- *have spare invitations ready in case*
  an extra child has to be invited
  unexpectedly

Drawn or painted invitations

Your child can draw, paint or stick
coloured bits of paper onto white or
coloured cards. If you want to have
recognizable pictures or designs on
the card you can cut or tear these
out yourself before letting the
children stick them on.

If the party is to have a theme it
is important that the picture on the
invitation indicates this.

Balloons

Write the invitations with a felt tip
pen on blown up balloons, and
draw a picture on the balloons as
well, if you wish. Once the ink is
dry let the balloons deflate and
stick them onto the invitation cards.
The children receiving the
invitations will then have to blow
up the balloons again before they
can read the words.

Collages

Older children can piece together a
collage by sticking paper, bits of
cloth, dried leaves or other
materials onto the invitations.

Potato printing

You can make all kinds of motifs in
different colours with a potato
stamp. You will need half a potato
for this (see p.66).

Rebus puzzles

Children aged about seven to nine
enjoy inventing riddles. Help your
child devise an invitation in the
style of a rebus (a puzzle in which
letters and pictures follow each
other in sequence to make a
sentence or message).

Jigsaw puzzle

You can often find photographs or
pictures relating to parties in old
magazines and you can stick them
onto blank cards. Write the words
on the back and then cut the cards
into jigsaw puzzle pieces.

The children have to fit the
pieces together again before they
can read the invitation.

Postcard invitations

If your child's party comes soon
after a vacation, you can choose a
few postcards while on vacation
and send them as a joint vacation
postcard and invitation.

Party hats

▶ *Stiff coloured or gold card, coloured paper, newspaper, coloured crayons and/or paints, a knife, some elastic and a stapler.*

Party hats give a cheerful and colourful look to a party. Each child receives a hat as they arrive or you can make and decorate the hats with the children during the party.

Crowns or headbands

- Have ready strips of coloured card 65 × 6 cm (25 × 2½ in). Attach the two ends to each other to form headbands.
- If you want to make crowns, cut out triangles along one side to make the points of the crown before joining the ends together.
- Add stickers to the headband or paint them. You can stick a figure such as the head of an animal onto the front (see Figure 1).

Cone-shaped party hats

Figure 2 shows some simple conical hats.

- Cut out a circle from stiff paper or card. A radius of 20 cm (8 in) will make a hat for a child. The smaller the radius the smaller the hat (see Figure 3).
- Cut two slits leading into the centre of the circle so that you can then cut out a segment. The smaller the cut-out segment, the flatter the hat will be.
- Alternatively you can cut the circle in half along the diameter. Then you can make a hat out of each semicircle. Bring the ends of the straight side together and stick the two edges together. Make two holes opposite each other at the bottom of the hat to take the elastic band.
- If you want a brim to the hat draw the circumference of the hat on a piece of card. Draw a second circle 5 cm (2 in) further out. Cut out the outer circumference but on the inside allow

15 mm (½ in) extra. Now make cuts 15 mm (½ in) deep into the inside to make flaps. Stick these flaps to the inside of the hat (Figure 4).

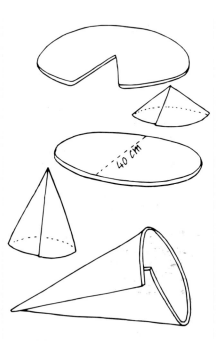

Figure 3

Figure 1

Figure 2

Figure 4

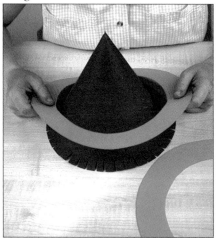

Sun shade

This can be in the style of a baseball cap and can be made in different colours for team games. Cut out the shape of the shade (see Figure 6). Draw or paint the theme of the party on one side and write the words on the other. Make a hole on both sides of the shade and attach an elastic band so that it can be worn. For team games you can make shades of two different colours.

A folded hat

- Fold a sheet of paper (50 × 40 cm, 20 × 16 in) in two as shown in Figure 5. Then fold again in two and open out the last fold again. Then fold points A and B to the centre.
- Fold the strips left over at the bottom towards the top, one strip on one side and the other on the other. Fold the triangles over which project beyond the slope of the hat and stick them to the opposite side (see Figure 5).

Variation:
With two extra folds you can alter the hat.
   Bring points C and D towards each other and fold point C to point E. Then open out the hat (see Figure 5f–5g).

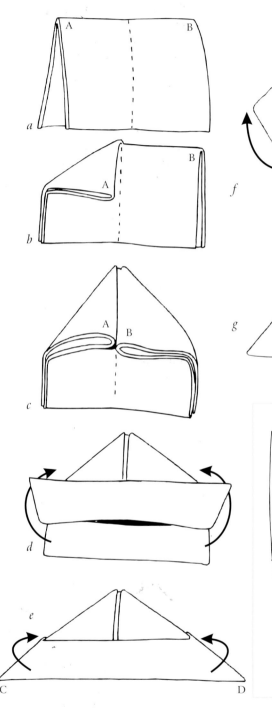

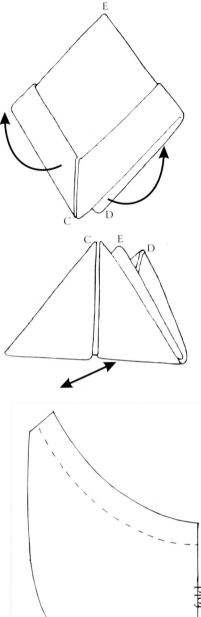

Figure 5

Figure 6 (50% of true size)

28

Paper chains and other decorations

It is easy to make paper chains. You will need plenty of long ones to decorate a whole room. It can be fun making these with children, even if you end up having to finish them off yourself. It will keep you busy for a good few afternoons or evenings.

Crêpe-paper chains

▶ *Crêpe-paper, glue, card, string*
You can buy various colours of crêpe-paper folded in a packet. Cut the folded paper into strips about 5 cm (2 in) wide. Now you will have little flat rolls of crêpe-paper.
- Make several cuts (about 1 cm, ½ in apart) into the open sides of the folds, to about one third of the width. Then unroll the strips and stick the ends together. Secure the ends of the chain by sticking them onto a piece of card.

- Twist the chain round lengthwise a few times so that the cuts open slightly. Make a hole in the card at the end of the chain and thread a piece of string through it so that the chain can be hung up (see Figure 7).

Two-colour chains
Lay two different coloured strips on top of each other and then twist them round each other (see p.31).

Paper ring chains

▶ *Coloured paper for folding, card*
Even very small children will enjoy making this chain.
- Cut the coloured paper into strips about 4 cm (1½ in) wide and 20 cm (8 in) long. (You can vary both the width and the length.) Stick the two ends together to make a loop.
- Thread the next strip of paper through the first loop and stick both the ends together again. Continue until the chain has reached the desired length (see Figure 8).

Paper boys or girls chains

▶ *Coloured paper, a piece of stiff paper*
- Cut strips of paper about 16 cm (6 in) wide and fold them concertina-fashion so that they measure about 12 cm (5 in) across.
- Fold a piece of stiff paper 16 × 12 cm (6½ × 5 in) in half lengthwise.
- Draw half a boy or girl on the folded paper, with the hands and feet extending to the edges (Figures 10 overleaf). Cut this figure out and unfold it. Now you have a pattern.
- Using the pattern draw the outline on the folded pack of paper. Cut the shape out of the pack without cutting the ends off the hands and feet. When you unfold the pack the children's hands and feet will be joined.
- Cut out several strips in the same way and attach them to each other till the chain has reached the desired length.
- If the chains are very long, run a thread through their centre. The chain will then hang from the thread and will not tear.

Figure 7

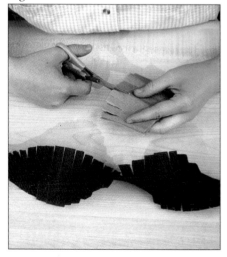

Figure 8

Figure 9

Variation: boys and girls chains

- Figure 10 shows a pattern of a figure that can become either a boy or a girl. (variations are dotted lines)
- Draw the outline of the pattern onto the folded pack of paper. Cut out along the outermost of the lines.
- Unfold the concertina and cut out the hair and skirt of the girl in the one figure and the trousers of the boy in the next. This will create a chain in which boy and girl alternate.

Figure 10 (70% of true size)

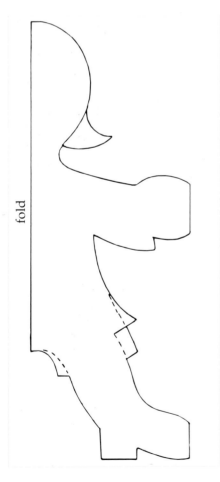

fold

Another variation:
You can make similar chains with different motifs, for example something relating to the party: an animal, a dragon's head, a witch, or the figure '8' if the birthday child is eight years old.

Folded paper chains

▶ *Sheets of paper for folding*
This chain is simple to make.
- Fold the sheets in half lengthwise and breadthwise.
- Make cuts into the folded sheets as shown in Figure 11.
- Unfold the sheets again and glue them on top of each other, sticking the first two sheets together by putting a bit of glue on the four outside corners, the second and third by sticking the centre pieces together, and so on (see picture at top of p.31).

Figure 11

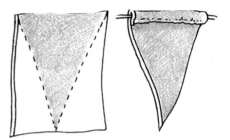

Figure 12

Flag chains

▶ *Thin string, coloured paper for folding*
- Cut the flags out from different coloured sheets of paper, 15 × 10 cm (6 × 4 in) or 20 × 15 cm (8 × 6 in) as shown in Figure 12.
- Stick the tops of the flags onto the string.

Bunches of balloons

Bunches of blown-up balloons can be very decorative, especially on the gate post of the house where the party will take place.

Paper flowers

▶ *Various colours of tissue paper, copper wire (0.8 mm, $^1/_{32}$in thick), glue, strong thread, wadding, a pair of small pointed pliers, thin wire (0.25–0.35 mm, $^1/_{64}$in).*
- For the stalk of the flower take a piece of copper wire, use the

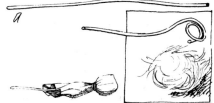

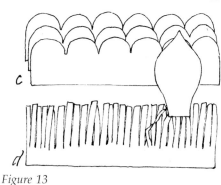

Figure 13

Figure 14

pliers to curl it round at one end (see Figure 13a) and wrap some wadding round it.

- Wrap a square piece of tissue paper round the blob of wadding and secure it underneath.
- For the petals cut out a strip from a sheet of tissue paper the same colour as the flower. The length of the strip determines the size of the flower. You might want to make it about 4–5 cm (1½–2 in). Keep folding the strip in half until you have the desired width of the petal. The width can vary from 2 to 4 cm (¾–1½ in).
- Cut a round or pointed shape along the narrow edge, or just

cut slits into the edge, depending on the shape you would like to have for the petals (Fig. 13b–d).

- Open out the petal and glue one end to the top of the stalk.
- Gather the petals into the place where the strip is glued and as you do so wrap the strip round the wire.
- Once the strip is fully wrapped round the wire secure the last end. Cut out another strip if the flower has too few petals.
- Tie the bottoms of the petals firmly to the stalk with strong thread and open out the petals at the top.
- Wrap some tissue paper round the stalk and if you wish stick on some leaves.

Home-made presents to take away

In Chapter 5 we mentioned little presents which the children could take home with them. Some of these are described under *Creative activities*, p.61.

The following instructions are for presents you can make yourself.

Felt gnome

▶ *Pipe cleaners, plain (unvarnished) wooden beads (diameter about 12 and 5 mm, ½ in and ¼ in), pieces of felt, unspun sheep's wool, thread, glue*

- Bend a pipe cleaner in half and insert the folded end into the hole of a bead with a diameter of 12 mm (½ in).
- Twist a second pipe cleaner horizontally round the first one to create arms at the place where the neck will be (Figure 16b). Cut these to size.

Figure 15

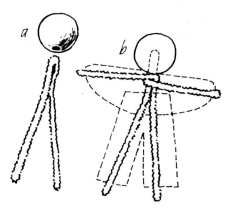

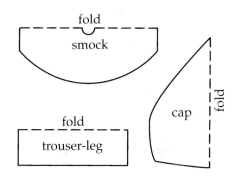

Figure 16

- Cut out two trouser legs from material folded double (Figure 16). Fold them round the legs and sew them together just below the arms to make trousers.
- Cut out the smock from the pattern and lay it round the doll's shoulders, then secure the arms and back.
- Cut out the pointed hat and sew the sides together. Stick some unspun wool onto the head for hair and onto the chin for a beard. Then stick the hat onto the head.
- Stick little beads onto the ends of the pipe cleaners to make hands and feet.

Home-made dipped candle

▶ *Beeswax or the remains of wax candles, candle wick, small narrow tins, a saucepan of hot water and a tea light or night light.*

You can make candles very successfully with children, but everyone has to be patient because the wax on the wick has to set before it can be dipped back into the melted wax.

- Put the wax or candle remains into a small narrow tin. Put this into a saucepan of boiling water on the stove and let the wax melt.
- Lay some newspaper on the table to absorb any spilt wax. When the wax is melted put the saucepan over a tea light or night light. The wax will gradually cool and stiffen so it is advisable to have a second tin of melted wax to work with in reserve.
- Cut a length of the candle wick and pull it taut with both hands.
- Dip the wick into the melted

Figure 17

wax for a moment, take it out and allow to cool and set before dipping it in again.

- If you take out the wick too soon very little wax will have stuck to it, but if you leave it in too long then any wax already on the wick will melt and disappear so that the candle becomes thinner instead of thicker.
- By alternately dipping and cooling you build up the candle layer by layer. The height of the tin determines the length of the candle. Once the candle is ready leave it some hours to cool properly and harden. Hang the candle up by the wick to avoid damaging it.

Woollen dolls

▶ *Thick knitting-wool in different colours, thread in various colours, stiff card*

- Wind the woollen yarn about twenty times round a piece of card about 6 cm (2½ in) wide to create arms. Secure the ends with a bit of thread. Pull the wool off

Figure 18

the card and tie up the hands about 1 cm (½ in) from each end.

- Wind the wool about forty times round a piece of card 8 cm (3 in) wide to create the head and trunk. Tie up one end of the woollen yarn where the head will be and then pull the wool off the card. Tie a knot about 2 cm (¾ in) below for the neck.
- Stick the arms through the loop of the upper part of the body under the neck and tie a knot around the waist.
- Decide whether the doll is to have a skirt or trousers. For a skirt the loops at the bottom must be cut open. For trousers the loops are divided into two equal parts which are tied up at the ends just like the hands.

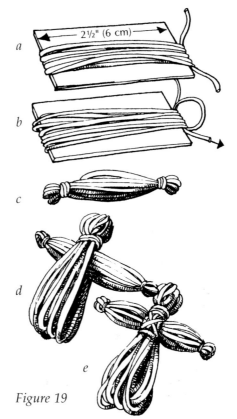

Figure 19

Window transparency

▶ *Stiff card coloured on one side, coloured tissue paper, dried leaves and grasses, transparent paper, starch or glue*

A transparency is a picture created on transparent paper. A beautiful effect is created when light shines through it. The picture could be part of a story you tell during the party, or you could depict something related to the season, for example you can make a lovely autumn transparency with grasses, little twigs and dried leaves (see Figure 20a).

Tissue paper window transparency

- Decide on the design of the transparency and draw it on the transparent paper.
- Tear or cut out the figures and scenes of the picture from the tissue paper and stick these onto the transparent paper with a little glue. If you build up layers

Figure 20

of different colours on top of each other you will create some beautiful effects.

- Cut out the transparency and stick it onto a frame of stiff card (see Figure 20a).

Table transparency

This transparency is made in exactly the same way as the window transparency, but it can stand on a table with a candle or small lamp behind it. To enable the transparency to stand you must make side panels as in a triptych. (See Figure 20b).

Cardboard basket

▶ *Thin card (for example, A4/legal)*
- Fold both sides of the card in half.
- Fold the two sides over once again to create sides for the basket. First bring up the long sides, and then bring up the two ends. Fold in the corners and if necessary glue them down.
- Now fold over the bits sticking out at each end and glue them down.
- Cut out a strip of card for a handle and glue this to the outer edges of the long sides (see Figure 21).

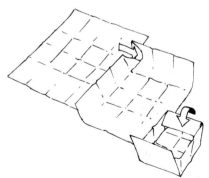

Figure 21

Pointed bag

▶ *Pretty wrapping paper*
The size of the paper depends on what is to be put into the bag. You can put about 200 g (7 oz) of little candies into a pointed bag made from a sheet of A4/legal size.
- Fold the top or bottom of the sheet diagonally so that it extends about 1 cm (½ in) over the lower side. Fold the protruding strip over and stick it to the base sheet with some glue.
- Cut off the superfluous paper.
- You can decorate the bag with a name label (Figure 22).

Paper napkins wrapping

▶*Paper napkins in various colours and/or designs*
Unfold two napkins and lay the corner of one on the right side of the other. If the napkins are the

Figure 23

same size you can use two different colours. Put a candy or other little present in the middle of the napkins and bring the edges together. Tie the packet up with a ribbon and attach a little label with the name of the child (Figure 23).

Figure 22

8 The Programme

Organizing the party

The general order of events for the party could be as follows:
- *unwrapping the presents*
- *a drink and something to eat*
- *introducing the theme of the party*
- *if necessary some games for the children to get to know each other*
- *games (some action games and some quieter ones)*
- *eating the birthday cake and tea*
- *the end of the party and getting ready to go home*

Receiving the youngest guests

After welcoming the children you can check with whoever has brought them when they will be collected. Some children need to be helped to take off their coats, and it is a good idea to remember where the coats have been put. Try to stuff hats and gloves into the relevant coats. Coat hangers with the names of each child will save a lot of hunting around at the end of the party.

If the party has a theme and the children have come in fancy-dress make a note of what they have brought with them. If you yourself have provided the costumes you can give them out when the children arrive.

If you are going to sit in a circle to give out the presents make sure all the children are brought to a chair.

Unwrapping the presents

- Don't wait too long for the presents to be unwrapped. The birthday child will be keen to know what the presents are and the other children will also be excited because they will want to watch the birthday child unwrap the present they have brought. If some children arrive late they can give their presents later, for example after the birthday cake.
- If the children arrive together after school they can sit down in a circle as soon as they come. If they all arrive separately you can have a table where they can put their presents when they come.
- Children find giving presents very important. Leave enough time so that all the children can see each present after it has been unwrapped, and then check that it has been put safely aside.

- To avoid the birthday child's best friends giving their presents first and other children feeling left out, you can plan a present giving order. A good way is to do this with a game.

Games for unwrapping presents
- The birthday child stands in the middle of the circle with their hands in front of their eyes. One of the children makes a noise. The birthday child has to guess who made the noise. If they guessed correctly then that child can give their present, but if not the next child makes a noise.
- The birthday child puts their hands in front of their eyes. All the other children give you something belonging to them, for example a shoe, hairslide or a badge. All the objects are put into a box or basket. Without looking the birthday child takes out one of the objects and the owner of that object can then give their present.
- Make two sets of identical cards beforehand. Keep one set on one side and put the other set into a basket. As each child arrives they take a card. When all the children are sitting down the birthday child takes a card out of the first set and the child who has the same card gives their present.

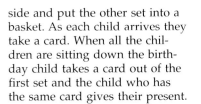

Games for getting to know each other

Although it doesn't matter very much with little children, children over five or six need to know each other's names. You will find suitable games on p.40.

Games for linking activities

These games (p.42) fill in time, for example while waiting for everyone to arrive or for the next event to happen. Simple games which don't require any materials are the best. You can explain the game in a few words, and the children can join in as soon as they arrive.

A meal

If the children all come straight from school and are hungry you can begin with the meal and then start on the presents afterwards.

Make sure that everything is ready. You can avoid problems by arranging the seating beforehand. Have cards with the name of the child by their place on the table. Alternatively write the names on a decorated table mat or stick a flag in a bread-roll or in an apple.

You might prefer to have the meal at the end of the party. If the children are going to be hungry when they arrive give them a small snack at the beginning and have a party meal at the end.

Eating the cake

There are various moments during the party when the cake can be brought in. It could be during a pause between games. If you are having a treasure hunt the cake could be brought in at the end of that. Or if you are having a birthday tea the cake could be the main focus.

Inside or outside?

If possible have some of the party outdoors. However, you will need to bear in mind that it takes a long time to get small children in and out of warm clothes, so if it is very cold you may not have much time. Children over five, on the other hand, will really enjoy the chance to be outside as well as inside. You can play all sorts of games outside which allow the children to run about.

Action games and quiet games

It is good to alternate action games with quiet games.

Active outdoor games include:
- *ball games*
- *group games and scouting games*
- *relay races*
- *catch and other outdoor games*

Quiet outdoor games include:
- *a number of circle games such as* I sent a letter to my love, *p.53*
- *blindfold games*

If the party is indoors it is easier to have quiet creative games and to make things. The occasional action game will then be a good diversion.
   Action games which can be played indoors are found under: *Action songs and games* (p.43), *Simple group games* (p.47) and *Active indoor games* (p.68)

List of games

It is a good idea to make a list of the games which you are going to play and the materials which you will need for them. As it is highly unlikely that the party will go entirely according to plan, it is useful to have some extra games in reserve. You may find that a certain game proves unpopular or too difficult. If there is a problem with a game don't press on regardless. See which games work well and what the children enjoy. Sometimes the children will want to repeat or carry on with one particular game and sometimes they will not want to play it at all. Games can also take longer than anticipated. For example, in *Hide and seek* it may take ages to find the last child.

Telling a story

A story is a good way of introducing a theme, or it can be used as a lead-in to a game or a treasure hunt. It is good if the story contains elements which feature in subsequent activities. You can also tell a story for its own sake, to create a calm interlude or to finish off the party. The story might refer to something that has happened during the party but it does not have to.

The art of story-telling used to be a natural part of every folk culture and tradition, but now we often have to relearn it and practise telling a story beforehand. You can read the story aloud from the book, but you have much more contact with your listeners if you tell it without a book, and you will be able to see their reactions immediately.

Preparing a story

If you know which book your children are reading or listening to you can look for stories relating to it or which are appropriate for the party. Once you have chosen the story, read it several times on successive days, so that you become familiar with its structure.

Make a note of the most important events of the story and remind yourself of these before you tell the story. If it would make you feel more confident you can make a copy of the story and mark the significant parts. You can then hold this copy of the story on your lap as you tell it.

Finishing the party

Sometimes a party ends abruptly once all the games have been played or it is time to go home. You can avoid this by working towards the end of the party so that it is nicely rounded off. It is better to cut out some of the games than to be pushed for time.

A good ending can be:
- a quiet game
- a short story
- just to sit and talk about what has happened at the party
- have something else to eat and drink

Making sure that all the children get home safely

If it is your responsibility to ensure that the children get home, you will need to have made proper arrangements with the parents so that no misunderstandings arise.

- *You can avoid problems by putting the finishing time on the invitation and making sure that you are aware of everyone's arrangements.*

Rehearsing beforehand

If you want to be sure that you have everything you need and know exactly where to find it you can run through the games which need materials. Check for instance whether you can see through the blindfold, whether the glue really sticks, that the sweets will not fall off the cake and so on. If you are going to bake something with the children, try out the recipe beforehand.

9 Games

Categories and Symbols

Age
As indicated in the text.

Number of players
4   Number of players
4⁺   Minimum number

If number not specified, any number can play.

Type of activity
O   Circle game
♦   Team game
✎   Paper and pencil
♪   Game with music
◐   Ball game

▶   What you need

Where to play
If not otherwise indicated, games are suitable for both indoors and outdoors.

Music
The symbol ♪ indicates that the game is accompanied by music, as in *Musical chairs* or *I saw two bears*. If you play an instrument you could provide the music. Otherwise you can play a CD.

What you will need
▶ indicates what equipment is required for a game or creative activity.

    At nearly every party you will also need a pair of scissors, a penknife, sticky tape, pencils, coloured crayons, felt-tips and paper.

Numbering-off games

One two, one two
Age 3–6 4⁺ ♦

The children stand in a circle or a line. If you need two teams number the children off, one two, one two. If you need three teams number them off one, two, three etc. The children with the same numbers go and stand in groups.

Bands or badges
Age 5–10+ 4⁺ ♦

▶ *Bands or badges*
Have a basket ready with bands, badges or other objects, in two or three different colours depending on how many teams you want to create. Each child takes an object out of the basket and joins the children who have picked the same colour.

Games for getting to know each other

What does Johnny look like?
Age 5–9

In this game one child has to describe what another child looks like. The first child turns round or puts their hands in front of their eyes. The second child then asks questions such as 'What colour eyes has Johnny got?' Each correct answer is followed by another question. When the child does not know the answer or gets it wrong it is the next child's turn.

How many beans?
Age 5–9 **5⁺**

▶ *Bags with fifteen to twenty beans*
This is a nice way for the children to get to know each other as they arrive.

As the children arrive they are each given a bag containing about fifteen beans. The children introduce themselves to each other in pairs then one of each pair holds out their closed hand with some beans in it. The other child asks 'Odds or evens?' Guided by the answer they then make a guess at the number of beans the first child is holding. If they guess correctly they win all the beans. If they are wrong they hand over the correct number of beans. It is then the second child's turn to hold the beans. When you say 'Time's up!' the children count up their beans to see who has won the most.

One potato, two potato
Age 5–9 **5⁺**

This can be used to identify one child who will perform some specific role.

The children stand in a circle and hold out both fists. Chant as follows:

One potato, two potatoes, three potatoes, four,

Five potatoes, six potatoes, seven potatoes, more.

Work your way round the circle tapping one fist on each word. The fist you tap on 'more' is out. Start the chant again and continue in the same way. When someone has lost both fists they are out. Continue until only one fist is left.

Tic-tac
Age 5–10+ **2 ♟**

Two children stand some distance apart. They take turns to put one foot exactly in front of the other. The player who closes the gap is the winner.

Connections
Age 5–10+ **4⁺ ♟**

▶ *Cards*
This is an original way of forming pairs. Write the names of famous people on half the cards. Then write or draw things belonging to those people on the other half. Everyone then receives a card and looks for their partner.

May I introduce myself?
Age 5–9 **4-8**

▶ *Drawing paper, pencils, coloured crayons*
This game works best with a maximum of eight children, otherwise it takes too long. As they arrive the children go and sit down at the table and draw something relating to themselves. When everyone has finished each child describes their picture (therefore saying something about themselves).

Remembering names
Age 5–9 **O**

This game works well at the beginning of a party when the children do not yet know each other.

Everyone stands in a circle and takes turns to say their first name. Then one child goes into the middle of the circle, points to another child and says 'left' or 'right.' The child who has been chosen must then say the name of the child on their left or right. If they do not know the name they must go into the middle.

Whose is this balloon?
Age 5–9 **5⁺ ♪**

▶ *Balloons, dark felt-tip pens*
Have ready plenty of balloons, already blown up. The children all write their names on a balloon. When the music starts they send their balloons up into the air one by one. As soon as the music stops, each child tries to catch a balloon. They then read the name on the balloon and see if they can identify whose it is. This game can be repeated several times.

Forfeits as a game for getting to know each other
Age 7–10+ **4⁺**

As each child arrives they hand over something as a forfeit, for example a bracelet, a scarf or a shoe. Everything is put into a box. You then take out a forfeit and ask the children what task the owner must perform in order to get their forfeit back. Before each child starts on their task they say their name.

The newspaper game
Age 7–10+ **5⁺ O**

▶ *Newspapers*
This is another useful game for learning names.

The children stand in a circle with one person in the middle with a long rolled-up newspaper. The game begins with one child in the circle calling out the name of another child in the circle. As soon as the name is called out the child in the middle tries to identify the child and touch them with the rolled-up newspaper (they are not allowed to touch the wrong child). If the named child manages to call out someone else's name before being touched, the child with the newspaper must then attempt to touch that child instead. When the child in the middle eventually manages to touch someone, that child takes over their role.

You can make it a little harder by requesting that a name may not be called out again until all the other names have been called.

Who am I?
Age 7–10+ **4⁺**

▶ *Bits of paper and sticky tape*
Stick a piece of paper with the name of a famous person onto each child's back. Everyone goes round asking questions to find out the name on their back. The answers can only be 'yes' and 'no.'

Who will stand next to me?
Age 7–10+ **8⁺ O**

The children stand in a circle with one gap. The child on the left of the gap begins. They look round the circle and say someone's name. That child has to go and stand in the gap. This will create a new gap and the child on the left of this gap now names another child to come and stand in it. Make sure that all the names are called out.

Games for linking activities

How many balls in the bucket?
Age 5–9 **3⁺**

▶ *Bucket, three tennis balls, tape or string*

Place a bucket on the ground about one metre (3 feet) from a wall. Place the tape about 3 metres (10 feet) front of the bucket. The distance can be greater for older children. The children try to throw the three tennis balls into the bucket. This is difficult as the balls often bounce out again. Say beforehand how many 'goes' each child can have and give one point for every ball that stays in the bucket.

Pick the raisin
Age 5–9 **3-8** *indoors*

▶ *Plate, raisins*

Put a plate of raisins on a table. One child goes out of the room. Another child points to one of the raisins on the plate. The child outside is called in again and picks up the raisins one by one. When they touch the raisin which the other child has pointed to everyone cries 'Stop!' The child keeps the raisins they have already taken and another child goes out of the room. Meanwhile the plate is filled with raisins again. The game goes on until everyone has had a turn. (If someone is unlucky and only gets a few raisins slip them some more).

The dark wood
Age 5–9 **7⁺** *indoors*

You need a big room for this game without obstacles.

One child goes and stands in a corner. The other children spread themselves round the room. The child in the corner looks where everyone is standing. They are then blindfolded and have to walk over to the opposite corner. They imagine they are in a dark wood and there are trees (other children) in the way. They must try to remember where the trees are and avoid bumping into them. The one who bumps into the least trees on their way across the room has won.

How many names?
Age 7–9 **3⁺** ✎ *indoors*

Say a first name, for example Anna, and get the children to write down as many names as they can beginning with the same letter, in this case A. You can also play this game with animals, plants, fruits, and so on.

Tongue-twisters
Age 5–9

These can be a fun way of filling in a few minutes while waiting for something else to happen. Practise the tongue-twisters well yourself beforehand. Then get the children to repeat them several times in succession as fast as possible. Some children can do this more quickly than others but it is not meant to be a race.

You can use short ones, such as 'Red lorry, yellow lorry' or whole sentences such as:

- *Stroppy sloppy soap is slowly stocking up the shop.*
- *Pretty Betty picks the prickly bricks.*
- *A noisy noise annoys an oyster.*
- *She sells sea shells on the seashore.*
- *Lazy Lizzy leaves a lot of lively lizards lying in a little loop.*

Action songs and games

Most of the games in this section involve actions and imitation as it is important for little children to have the chance to move about. They love playing games in which they imitate all kinds of movements. Sometimes they can provide the action themselves. You can help by whispering suggestions to them.

In fine weather these games can be played out of doors.

Follow my leader
Age 3–4 **3⁺** ♪

This is a simple game which you can use to take the children to the play area or to a place where you are going to play another game.

The children link hands to make a chain. Take the leading child's hand and lead the chain through the room, or if you are playing the game outside lead them through the trees and round the flower beds. The birthday child might like to lead the train.

For the second and third verses the children imitate your actions. You can make up more verses to suit the occasion.

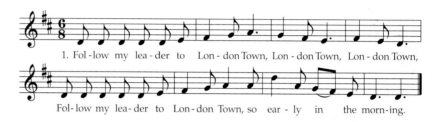

1. Fol-low my lea-der to Lon-don Town, Lon-don Town, Lon-don Town,
Fol-low my lea-der to Lon-don Town, so ear-ly in the morn-ing.

2. *Play on your drum to London Town, London Town, ...*

3. *Play on your violin to London Town, London Town, ...*

The mulberry bush
Age 3–6 **3⁺** O ♪

The children dance round in a circle imitating your actions. For the first verse simply dance round until the line 'On a cold and frosty morning' when you stop and rub you arms to keep warm.

On the second verse, make the actions of washing hands. Then wash clothes in a tub, hang them up to dry on a line, sweep the floor with a brush, and brush your hair.

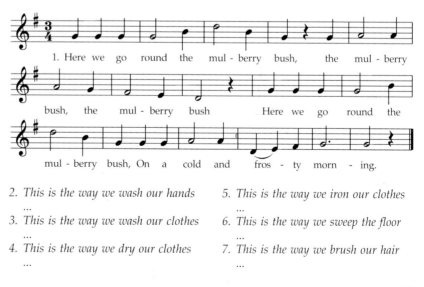

1. Here we go round the mul-berry bush, the mul-berry bush, the mul-berry bush Here we go round the mul-berry bush, On a cold and fros-ty morn-ing.

2. *This is the way we wash our hands ...*

3. *This is the way we wash our clothes ...*

4. *This is the way we dry our clothes ...*

5. *This is the way we iron our clothes ...*

6. *This is the way we sweep the floor ...*

7. *This is the way we brush our hair ...*

The grand old Duke of York
Age 3–6 **4⁺ O ♪**

The children stand in a circle and march on the spot, singing along with you.

On the word 'up' the children stretch up as high as they can and on the word 'down' they crouch down low. On the last phrase they kneel down and reach up at the same time.

Once they have the idea they can sing the song and do the actions while marching round in a circle.

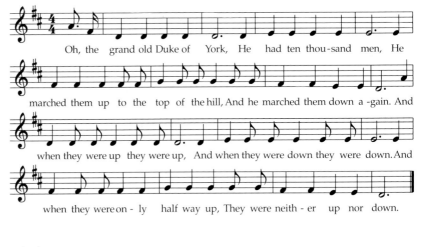

Can you plant your cabbages
Age 3–6 **4⁺ O ♪**

The children stand in a circle singing.

On the second and third verses they stamp with their feet and pat with their hands at the appropriate time.

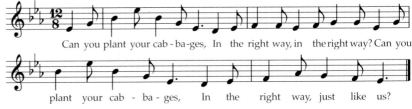

2. *You can plant them with your foot*
   In the right way, ...

3. *You can plant them with your hand*
   In the right way, ...

London Bridge is falling down
Age 3–6 **6⁺ O ♪**

The children skip and sing going under the arch formed by two children, until the verse 'Here's a prisoner ...' when the pair making the arch catch one of the children. The prisoner has to remain captive to the end of the song, when it can be repeated with a new pair forming the arch.

Iron bars will bend and bow ...
Build it up with pins and needles ...
Pins and needles will rust and bend ...
Build it up with penny loaves ...
Penny loaves will tumble down ...
Here's a prisoner I have got ...

What's the prisoner done to you ...
Stole my watch and broke my chain ...
What'll you take to set him free ...
Ten hundred pounds will set him free ...
Ten hundred pounds we have not got ...
Then off to prison he must go ...

44

The big ship sails
Age 5–6 **6⁺** ♪

The children hold hands in a line. The child at the end makes an arch against a wall. The child at the other end leads the line under the arch until the child forming the arch is twisted round crossing their arms. The leader then then goes through the next arch so the next child twists round as the last one goes through. Repeat the first verse until all children have crossed their arm. Then the fist and last child join hands to join a circle and sing the second verse very slowly. On the third verse shake heads. On the fourth crouch down and rise again. Finally bend heads low.

Gathering nuts in May
Age 5–6 **6⁺** ♪

Form two lines facing each other. On verse 1 both lines skip forward then back. On verse 2 one line advances asking the question, the other line steps forward on verse 3 with the answer. Repeat for verses 4 and 5. The chosen two have a tug of war until the loser is pulled over to the other side.

Wallflowers
Age 3–6 **5⁺** O ♪

The children dance slowly round the circle holding hands. When a child is named, they turn around so they face the out of the circle. They still link hands and dance around. The song is repeated until all the players face out.

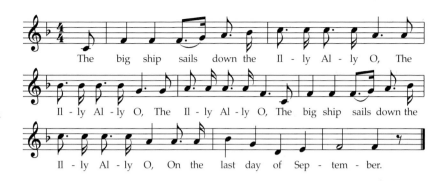

2. *The big ship sails too slow, too slow,*
   Too slow, too slow, too slow, too slow
   The big ship sails too slow, too slow,
   On the last day of September.

3. *The Captain said, 'It will never,*
   never do, ...

4. *The big ship sank to the bottom of*
   the sea, ...

5. *We all dip our heads in the deep*
   blue sea, ...

2. *Who will you have for nuts in May?*

3. *We'll have .... for nuts in May*

4. *Who will you send to fetch her away?*

5. *We'll have .... to fetch her away*

Oats and beans and barley

Age 3–6 **4⁺ ○ ♪**

The children link hands and dance round in a circle with the farmer in the middle during the chorus. On the first verse mime the words of the farmer. The chorus is repeated after the verse.

Ring, a ring o' roses

Age 3–4 **3⁺ ○ ♪**

The children link hands and dance round in a circle. On the word 'down' everyone falls to the floor.

A ship sailed from China

Age 5–9 **4⁺ ○ ♪**

This game is harder to keep up than first appears! Sit on the floor in a circle, legs straight in front. On the words 'like this' swing your right hand out to the right and then back to your lap, and keep repeating this action as you sing the song for a second time. At the end of the second time, additionally swing your left arm out left and back to your lap. After the third time your right leg joins the action, then your left leg, and finally on the fifth singing you head nods in time with all the other actions of the song.

46

Simple group games

Most of these games work best indoors, but you could also play some of them in a sheltered garden.

Biting the cake
Age 3–6

▶ *Cord, thin string, slices of cake (one slice for each child) or donuts*
Hang a piece of cord from one end of the room to the other, or between two trees. Tie a thin string around each slice of cake or donut, then tie the string to the cord so that the slices of cake or donuts hang down at about the height of the children's mouths.

Now everyone stands by a slice of cake or donut and puts their hands behind their backs. They all try to take a bite out of their slice of cake or donut. The first to eat all their slice of cake or donut without using their hands is the winner. Give a bit of help to anyone who is not managing to get a bite at all!

Sardines
Age 3–9 **5⁺**

One child hides then all the others go and look for them. When anyone finds the first child they say nothing and try to squeeze quietly into the hiding place without the others noticing. The game continues with more and more sardines getting into the tin, until the last child finds them all.

If outside, define the area that can be used.

Bon appetit!
Age 5–9 **5⁺** *indoors*

▶ *Knife and fork, a bar of chocolate, gloves and a dice*
Choose a child to start. This child has to put on the gloves and unwrap the bar of chocolate with the knife and fork. They then cut a piece off and try to eat it with the knife and fork. Meanwhile the others throw the dice in turn. The first to throw a six gets the gloves and the knife and fork and gets on with the job!

Who has the most squares?
Age 5–6 **2-6** *indoors*

▶ *A dice (an ordinary one, or one with different coloured sides) a sheet of paper, coloured crayons, counters*
Draw a square and divide it into 36 squares. The aim is to get as many squares as possible. You can play the game with an ordinary dice. With children who cannot yet count you can play with a dice with different colours on each side.

With a coloured dice:
Colour six of the squares on the paper red, six green and so on so that there are six squares for each of the six colours of the dice.

Give each child a different set of counters (for example, white beans, brown beans, peas, or coloured candy). The children take it in turns to throw the dice and put one of their counters onto one of the squares of the colour they have thrown. When all the squares of one colour are full a child who throws that colour again misses their turn. When all the squares have been filled the child who has claimed the most squares has won.

With an ordinary dice:
Write the figure 6 in six of the squares anywhere on the paper, then the figure 5 in six other squares, and so on. Everyone has a different coloured crayon and they take it in turn to throw the dice. They then colour one of the squares showing the number they threw on the dice. When all the squares showing one number are full a child who throws that number again misses their turn. At the end, the child who has coloured in the most squares is the winner.

Balloons
Age 5–9

▶ *Balloons, little presents, tiny pieces of paper*

Make as many presents as there are children and wrap them up. Stick numbers or labels on the packages. Put the same number or label on tiny pieces of paper and put each piece of paper into a balloon. Blow the balloons up and toss them into the air at the end of the party. Each child grabs a balloon and bursts it to retrieve the piece of paper which identifies their present.

Straw football
Age 5–9 **6⁺** 🙌 *indoors*

▶ *Table tennis ball, thin card, sticky tape, straws*

Stick long thin pieces of card round the table so that they stick up above the edge of the table. Leave an opening of about 15 cm (6 in) in the middle of each end to make goals. The children have to try to score a goal by blowing the ball along with their straws. If they touch the ball with the straw it counts as a foul and it is the next player's turn.

Flying animals
Age 5–9 **3⁺** *indoors*

▶ *Newspapers*

Each child cuts out (or tears out) the shape of an animal from a half sheet of newspaper. Everyone then lays their animals on the floor along one side of the room and gets a newspaper.. When the race begins, the children try to blow their animals along by waving their newspapers. The first one to get their animal to the opposite side of the room is the winner.

Telephone whispers
Age 5–9 **5⁺** ◯ *indoors*

This is a useful game for quietening noisy children.

Stand the children in a circle. Whisper something in the ear of the first child. It might be a made-up word, a simple sentence, or something funny. The first child then whispers the message to the second one and so on. No one is allowed to repeat what they have whispered. The last child then says out aloud what they heard, and usually it is something quite different from the original message.

Lucky dip
Age 3–9

▶ *Wrapped-up presents, a tin or box containing bits of packing-foam*

Put the presents in the box and let each child dip for their present before they go home.

Hot potato

Age 5–9 **6⁺ O** *indoors* ♪

▶ *Potato or ball*

This game works on the principle that you cannot hold a hot potato in your hand for long or you will get burnt, so you have to pass it on as quickly as possible. As the music plays the children pass the potato round the circle. They need to pass it quickly as whoever is holding the potato when the music stops is out. (The children have to imagine that the cold potato or ball they pass around is really an extremely hot potato).

Variation:

Instead of being out when they are left holding the potato, the children have to pass it on in an unusual way, such as under their legs, behind their back or on their knees.

How many things go into a box?

Age 5–9 **3-8** *indoors*

▶ *Lots of little objects, such as paper-clips, buttons, tiny stones, a little packet or container the same size for each child (for instance, an empty film canister, an empty matchbox)*

Put all the little objects on the table. Each child has an empty box or packet and they have five minutes in which to put as many objects into their box as they can. The box must not overflow and they must be able to close it. The person who gets the most things into their box is the winner.

Don't laugh

Age 5–9 **5⁺** *indoors*

Two children sit down on the floor opposite each other and try to make each other laugh by making funny faces or saying funny things. As soon as one of them laughs they are out, and another child takes their place.

Donkey's tails

Age 5–9

▶ *Empty bottles, string, nails*

Tie the nails onto the ends of pieces of string. Tie the pieces of string round the children's waists. The ends of the string should hang over the children's backs with the nails reaching down to the backs of their knees. When you say 'go' each child goes and stands in front of a bottle and tries to get their nail into the neck of the bottle.

They will only succeed if they manage to get the nails to hang between their knees.

Paying forfeits

Age 5–9 **5⁺** *indoors*

The children must give up a forfeit when they cannot answer a question, lose at a game, or do something wrong. The forfeit is something belonging to them such as a handkerchief, a comb or a hairslide. There are lots of games in which children have to pay forfeits, for example:

- *Earth, water, air, (p.54)*
- *All birds can fly (p.54)*
- *You must not say 'uhm' (p.60)*
- *Fizz Buzz (p.55)*
- *Who sinks the ship? (p.50)*
- *Spin the plate (p.75)*

If there are still some children left who have not paid a forfeit you can play:

- *Winkie (see p.53)*
- *Simon says (p.56)*
- *You may not answer 'yes' or 'no' (see p.60)* This is a variation on *You must not say 'uhm'*

The children have to carry out a task to retrieve their forfeits (see *Redeeming forfeits* overleaf).

Redeeming forfeits

Age 5–9 **5⁺**

The aim of this game is for everyone to win back their forfeits.

One child turns round and holds their hands in front of their eyes so that they cannot see the forfeits on the table. Another child points to a forfeit and asks what the owner must do to regain it. The child with their eyes covered must think up an amusing task without knowing who has to do it.

Examples of tasks:

- sing a song
- give someone a kiss
- hop round in a circle
- walk round the table with a book on their head
- get something nice from the kitchen for everyone to eat
- imitate an animal
- crawl through a tunnel of other children's legs
- act out something from a pantomime

Hunt the thimble

Age 5–9 **5⁺** *indoors*

▶ *A small object*
Show a small object (for example a table tennis ball or a thimble) to the children and then ask them all to go out of the room while you place the object somewhere where it can be seen but is not obvious. Explain that the object is not hidden inside anything, so that they do not start opening drawers and cupboards.

When you say 'ready' the children come back in and start looking. If someone sees the object they don't say anything but they stop looking. The game goes on until everyone has seen the object.

Hot or cold

Age 5–9 **5⁺** *indoors*

▶ *Something to hide*
One of the children goes out of the room and the others hide the object. Then the child outside is called in and starts looking for it. The others say 'hot' when the child is getting very near, and 'warm,' 'lukewarm,' 'cold,' or 'freezing' depending on how close they are to it. When the object has been found it is the next child's turn.

Who sinks the ship?

Age 5–9 **3⁺**

▶ *Basin, lids, teaspoons, dice*
Float some lids (for instance, jam-jar lids) in water inside a basin. The children throw the dice in turn. When someone throws a six they pour a teaspoonful of water into one of the lids. The lids get fuller and fuller so that in the end they sink. The child who is filling a lid when it sinks is out. The child who stays in longest is the winner.

Musical statues

Age 7–9 **4⁺** ♪ *indoors*

Everyone dances and hops round in a circle while music plays. As soon as the music stops everyone has to freeze. Anyone who then moves is out.

You can make the game more interesting by asking the children to freeze in specific shapes, for instance, as an elephant or a mouse, or curled up like a ball.

Fishing

Age 7–10+ **5⁺** *indoors*

▶ *Newspaper, string*
The children each cut out a fish from a quarter of a sheet of newspaper. Make a hole in each fish and tie a piece of string to it. Tie the other end of the string to the child's waist so that the fish trails behind them.

The aim is to catch a fish by treading on someone else's fish and tearing it off its string while at the same time keeping your own fish from being trodden on. The one who keeps their fish longest is the winner.

Circle games

The farmer's in the den
Age 3–6 **7⁺ ○ ♪**

Young children love singing this song. Someone is chosen to be the farmer and the other children walk in a circle around the farmer, holding hands and singing.

The farmer then chooses another child to come into the middle to be the wife. And then on each verse the last child to go into the middle chooses the next one. On the last verse all the children pat the child who is the dog, gently!

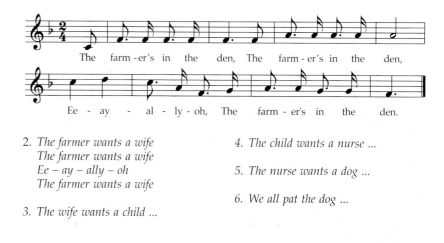

2. *The farmer wants a wife*
   The farmer wants a wife
   Ee – ay – ally – oh
   The farmer wants a wife

3. *The wife wants a child ...*

4. *The child wants a nurse ...*

5. *The nurse wants a dog ...*

6. *We all pat the dog ...*

Round and round the village
Age 5–6 **6⁺ ○ ♪**

The children stand in a circle while one child goes round the outside. In the second verse the child weaves in and out of the circle. Then the child's faces a partner, and in the next verse the pair skip around the outside of the circle; finally they shake hands.

The partner then begins anew.

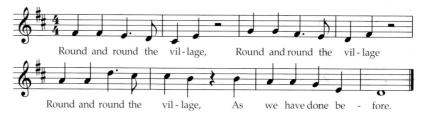

2. *In and out the windows ...*
   As we have done before.

3. *Stand and face your partner ...*
   As we have done before.

4. *Take her/him up to London ...*
   As we have done before.

5. *Shake hands before you leave her/him ... As we have done before.*

51

I sent a letter to my love
Age 5–9 **7⁺ O ♪**

▸ *Envelope or handkerchief*
The children sit in a circle facing inward. One of the children walks round behind the circle until they lay an envelope or handkerchief quietly behind one of the sitting children. When they finish the chant the children turn round to see if they have the envelope. The one who has, jumps up quickly and tries to catch the child who put it there before they sit down in the empty place. If they succeed, the other child now takes the envelope and the game begins again. If they are caught, they must go round with the envelope again.

Busy bees
Age 5–9 **7⁺ O**

This game only works with an uneven number of children. The children are paired off, leaving one child alone. This child faces the pairs and gives orders such as 'sit back to back' or 'hold hands.' But when they say 'busy bees' everyone has to change partners and the single child tries to find a partner. The child who fails to get a partner now has to give the instructions.

Three's too many!
Age 5–9 **12⁺ O**

The children stand in a double circle. Two children run round the outside circle with one trying to catch the other. The one being chased can run and stand in front of a child in the inside circle. *Three's too many,* and so the child standing behind in the outside circle must run from the catcher.

I sent a letter to my love And on the way I dropped it. One of you has picked it up and put it in your pock-et. Ah-choo, ah-choo, ah-choo.

Variation:
Instead of the pairs standing one behind the other, they hold their partner's hand, leaving each with one free hand. This time the child being chased can grab another child's free hand, either on the inside or the outside, and the child holding the other hand then has to run away.

52

Cat and mouse
Age 5–9 **12⁺ O**

One child is chosen to be the cat and two or three more are chosen to be mice, depending on the number of players. The other players stand in a circle holding hands. They let the mice run through but they try to prevent the cat from getting through. The cat must try to catch the mice as they dart out of and around the circle. Once the cat has caught all the mice it is the turn of a new cat and mice.

Poor Kitty
Age 7–10+ **8⁺ O**

One child is chosen to be a wily cat, and the other children sit in a circle. Kitty now goes and settles down in front of one of the children and begins to miaow pitifully. The child must then stroke Kitty and comfort her without smiling, saying 'Poor Kitty, poor Kitty.' But Kitty gets more and more worked up and tries to make the comforter laugh by doing all sorts of exaggerated cat actions. If the comforter does laugh they become 'Poor Kitty.'

Rush hour
Age 5–9 **8⁺ O** *indoors*

The children sit on chairs in a circle. In the middle stands a policeman controlling the traffic. He orders the children to change places by saying something like 'People with black shoes change places with people with red socks' or 'Trousers change places with dresses.' Rush hour starts and the policeman tries to sit on an empty seat. The person without a seat then becomes the policeman.

Passing the ring
Age 5–9 **8⁺ O**

▶ *String, a ring*
Pass a long piece of string through a ring and tie the ends together making sure that the ring can slip over the knot. The string must be long enough to go round the circle of children. One child goes into the middle of the circle and puts their hands in front of their eyes. The other children hold the string and one child has the ring in their hand. The child in the middle can now open their eyes. Everyone then pretends that they are passing the ring to the person on their right, while the child with the ring actually does pass it. The child in the middle has to guess who has the ring. If they guess correctly they change places with the person who had the ring.

Telephoning
Age 5–9 **8⁺ O**

Everyone stands in a circle holding hands except for one child who stands in the middle. One of the children in the circle chooses the name of a child on the other side of the circle and says, for example 'I'm going to phone Peter' and presses their neighbour's hand very gently. The neighbour presses their next neighbour's hand, and so on in the same way until Peter's hand is reached, at which point Peter shouts 'Peter speaking.' The idea is to make the hand pressure so slight that the child in the middle does not notice it. As soon as they spot a hand movement they call out the name of the person doing it and change places with them. It is then their turn to phone someone else.

Winkie
Age 7–10+ **9⁺ O**

You need plenty (but an odd number) of children for this to work well. Half the children sit on chairs in a circle, leaving one chair empty. The others stand behind the chairs with one child behind the empty chair. This child now tries to attract one of the sitting children to their chair by winking at them so secretly that the child behind them does not notice. They must try to move to the empty chair, but if the child behind notices they touch the shoulder of the escaping child who is then not allowed to move. If they get away the child behind the chair now has to wink, but if they fail the original one tries to find another partner. After a while change the teams round so that the standing team is now sitting and vice versa.

Cat and dog
Age 7–10+ **8⁺ O** *indoors*

▶ *Two small objects*
One child has two small objects. They give one to the child on their right saying 'This is a dog!'
That child then asks 'A what?'
The first child answers 'A dog.'
The second child then passes the object to the next child on *their* right and the conversation is repeated. The object continues round the circle in this way.
Meanwhile the first child gives the other object to the child on their left saying 'This is a cat!'
'A what?' asks the child on the left.
'A cat.'
Soon the cat and the dog meet and confusion begins. Anyone who mixes up the answers is out.

Memory, observation, word and guessing games

Earth, water, air
Age 5–9 **8⁺ ○ ◐** *indoors*

The children stand in a circle. One has a ball and throws it to another child. As they do so they call out one of the three elements: earth, water, or air. The child who catches the ball then has to call out an animal which lives in that element. If for instance 'air' is called they might answer 'sparrow.' If a child cannot answer or answers incorrectly they are out or have to pay a forfeit. Each animal can only be named once.

All birds can fly
Age 5–9 **5⁺ ○**

Stand in a circle with the children or ask them to form a line facing you. Begin the game by saying 'Allbirds can fly,' flapping your arms. The children copy you. Then name different sorts of birds such as 'All hawks can fly' flapping your arms each time. Then suddenly say an animal which cannot fly, for example 'All horses can fly.' Anyone who flaps their arms, or even lifts them, must pay a forfeit.

When you play the game with older children one of the children can take your role.

Jobs
Age 5–9 **5⁺ ○ ◐**

The children sit in a circle and one of them has a ball. They roll the ball to another child and call out a job. The child who picks up the ball must then name three things belonging to that job. For example if 'gardener' is called, they could say 'spade, hoe and rake.'

If the child takes too long to answer or the answers are wrong the ball goes back to the first child to be rolled to someone else.

Tools of the trade
Age 5–9 **5⁺** *indoors*

Prepare a story about a particular job, mentioning many of the tools used in that trade. Give each child the name of one of the tools. When you mention one of the tools in the story, the child with that tool has to shout 'mine!'

You can make the game more difficult by mentioning several tools one after the other. If a child forgets to call 'mine' they lose a point. The child with the least number of penalty points has won.

Animal, plant or mineral
Age 5–10+ **3⁺** *indoors*

One of the children thinks of an animal, a plant or an inanimate object. The others ask (either in turn or in any order) 'Is it an animal, a plant or a mineral?' The child must say which it is. After that the others ask questions to which the child can only answer 'yes' or 'no.' The one who calls out the right animal, plant or mineral thinks of the next one.

54

How many sticks?

Age 5–9 **3⁺** *indoors*

▶ *Cocktail sticks*

Tip a specific number of small sticks or cocktail sticks onto the table in a heap. The players take it in turns to guess how many sticks are in the heap. The one who guesses right or is the nearest scores three points, the next best two, and the one after that, one. Repeat the procedure with a different number of sticks each time until you want to end the game and then add up the scores. The player with the most points is the winner.

I spy with my little eye

Age 5–9 **3⁺** *indoors*

One of the children chooses something they can see and says, for example 'I spy with my little eye something that's red' or whatever the colour of the object. The other children then have to guess what the thing is.

I'm going on a journey

Age 5–9 **5⁺** *indoors*

The first starts by saying, for example 'I'm going on a journey and I'm taking a bag.' The next child then says 'I'm going on a journey and I'm taking a bag and a swimsuit.' The next child repeats the sentence and adds something. Each subsequent child must repeat all the previous children's things in the correct order each time adding something else. When someone makes a mistake they are out.

Ten letters

Age 7–10+ **3⁺** ✎ *indoors*

The children take it in turn to say a letter until there is a total of ten letters. Tell them that there must be about the same number of vowels as consonants as otherwise you cannot make a word. Everyone writes the letters down then they all try to make as many words out of the letters as possible.

What have I bought?

Age 5–9 **4⁺** *indoors*

One of the children thinks of something they have bought, for example a cucumber. Then they say to the others, 'I went to the shop and I bought something, but I've forgotten what it's called.' The other children then ask questions to try to guess what it is, for example 'Is it something to eat?' 'Is it red?' 'Is it expensive?' and so on. The questions can be answered with 'yes' and 'no.' The one who guesses the answer first has the next turn.

Who is it?

Age 5–9 **3⁺** ✎ *indoors*

This is a guessing game for children who already know each other well. Each child is given a sheet of paper on which they write a number of things about themselves such as their favourite food, their hobby, their favourite pop group and so on. You may want to determine beforehand what kind of things can be written down.

The children fold up the pieces of paper and put them in a basket. The papers are well shuffled and each child then takes out one of the pieces of paper and reads out what it says. Everyone then tries to guess who the writer is.

Fizz Buzz

Age 5–9 **5⁺**

In this game you are not allowed to say a number containing a seven or a multiple of seven (for example 27 or 21).

The first child says 'one,' the second 'two' and so on until the sixth child says 'six.' The next child must say 'eight.' If anyone makes a mistake they are out. The game goes on until only one child is left.

Easier variation:
An easier variation is to focus on the number five instead of seven.

More challenging version:
A more challenging version is to substitute the word 'Fizz' for a number containing a five or a multiple of five. If the children are feeling confident and ambitious you can add a further rule; to substitute 'Buzz' for numbers containing a seven or a multiple of seven. Any numbers containing both a five and a seven or which are multiples of both these numbers are substituted by 'Fizz Buzz.'

Simon says
Age 7–10+ **3⁺**

The children all sit around a table. You, or one of the children if they are old enough, then do a series of actions. There are seven actions illustrated alongside. When you say 'Simon says: Bowl' everyone has to copy. But if you omit 'Simon says' then everyone must keep still. To confuse everyone more, you can say, for example, 'Simon says: Flat' remaining still, or even doing something else yourself. The players must only do what 'Simon' says.

Do this, do that
Age 5–10+ **3⁺** **O**

In this similar game the children all sit in a circle. When you say 'Do this' everyone copies your action but when you say 'Do that' they must remain still. Anyone doing the wrong thing is out.

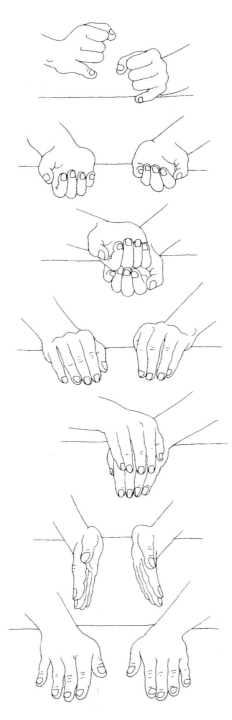

From top: pinkie; bowl; double bowl; bump; double bump; clap; flat

Detective
Age 7–10+ **4⁺** *indoors*

One of the children is the detective and they go out of the room. While they are out the others choose the chief criminal. When the detective comes back in the chief does various actions which the children copy as quickly as they can so that it is not easy to see who did the movements first. The detective has to try to find out who the chief is.

Advertisements
Age 7–10+ *indoors*

Each player has a sheet of paper and a pencil. Tell them to write the name of a food or product to be advertised. They can make something up if they wish. After writing this, everyone folds over what they have written and passes the sheet on to their neighbour. Without looking at what is written, you then give further instructions as to what to write, such as a description, instructions for use, the price, the shop where it can be obtained etc. Each time the sheet is folded over and passed on. When all the stages have been written the children unfold the papers and read out the advertisements.

Story variation
You can play the same game with a story. Each child writes a sentence and folds over the paper so that only the last word of the sentence is showing. They then pass their paper to their neighbour, who continues the story from the last word, again leaving only their last word showing.

Drawing variation
Everyone draws a head (of any kind) and folds the paper over so that only the neck shows. The next person draws the upper body and arms, the next person the lower body and hands, the next the legs and the last person the feet.

Consequences
Everyone writes a boy's name, folds their paper so that their writing does not show and passes it to the next person. The next person writes a girl's name and again folds and passes on the paper. The game continues in the same way everyone writing:
- the place where they met
- what he said to her
- what she said to him
- what the consequence was (e.g. they got married, they went swimming etc.)

Lots of lions in London
Age 7–10+ indoors

Everyone takes it in turn to think of three words beginning with the same letter and make a sentence containing those three words. For example, 'There are *lots* of *lions* in *London*' or 'My *brother bought* some *bread*.'

Variation: May I introduce myself
In this game everyone introduces themselves. They make up a sentence in which their name, job and home begin with the same letter. For example, 'I'm Diana, a doctor from Detroit' or 'I'm Billy, a builder from Birmingham.'

Changing clothes
Age 7–10+ **5⁺** *indoors*

▶ *Various clothes*
Pile a heap of different kinds of clothes in the middle of the room. Everyone puts on an article of clothing, except for one child who must watch carefully to see who has put on what. They then go out of the room and everyone swaps their clothes. When the child outside comes back in they have to say who was wearing which clothes before the change. The more children there are the harder this is. If you repeat the game more than twice bring in a new set of clothes otherwise it becomes too easy.

Teapot
Age 7–10+ **6⁺**

Two children go out of the room and choose a word with two meanings such as *train*. They call this word *teapot*. When they come back into the room they begin a conversation using the word in both its meanings. One child might say:
'My brother just caught the last teapot.' and the other might say, 'And my brother wants to teapot my dog properly.'
They continue like this until the others have guessed the word.

Whose case are we packing?
Age 7–10+ **5⁺** ✎ *indoors*

Explain to the children that they are going to pretend to pack a suitcase. One of the children goes out of the room and the others decide who the suitcase is for. One by one they say something which is to go into the suitcase and write it on a piece of paper. The papers are then folded and put in a bowl.
The child comes back in and takes a piece of paper from the bowl. They read it and try to guess who the suitcase has been packed for. If they don't know they take

out another piece and so on until they guess correctly. Then the next player goes out of the room. The winner is the one who refers to the least number of pieces of paper before they get the answer.

Who are you?
Age 7–10+

One of the children thinks of a person, and the others take turns asking questions to find out who the person is. The questions can only be answered with 'yes' or 'no.' After a 'yes' answer the person who asked the question can ask again, but after a 'no' answer it is the next player's turn. Anyone who thinks they know the identity of the mystery person can say straight away without waiting for their turn. Whoever guesses correctly is the next to think of a person.

Quiz
Age 7–10+ **ṀṀ** *indoors*

▶ *List with questions*
You need two or more teams for a quiz. Prepare a list of questions beforehand. You can use two types of questions, factual ones such as 'What is the capital of Japan?' 'What is the name of the President?' and riddles such as 'What holds water but is full of holes?' [A sponge]. 'What glove will not fit your hand?' [A foxglove]. You should be able to find quiz books in your local library.

Ask each team a question in turn. If the team answers correctly it scores two points. If it does not know the answer or gets it wrong the other team can then try. They

score one point if they get the answer. Decide beforehand how long the teams can have to answer each question. The team with the highest number of points wins.

Variation 1:
The questions are put to both teams simultaneously. The first child to raise their hand is allowed to answer. If they get it wrong the other team is allowed to try.

Variation 2:
Give both teams a list of the same questions. You can then give one point for every correct answer and five points to the team which finishes first.

Journey with obstacles
Age 10+ **4⁺** *indoors*

One child goes out of the room and thinks up the story of a journey. At the same time all the other children think of a word and everyone tells their word to everyone else. The storyteller comes back in and begins their story, every so often pointing to one of the children. That child then says their word and the storyteller must bring that word into their story. The story then has to take several unexpected and often amusing turns.

Peaceful games

Blowing bubbles
Age 3–6

▶ *Wire, dishwashing liquid, or ready-made bubble mixture*
You can buy ready-made tubs of bubble mixture but you can also use ordinary dishwashing liquid. Not all types of dishwashing liquid work well: the more concentrated they are the more they have to be diluted, so experiment beforehand.

To make a blower bend a piece of wire into a ring (about 2 cm, 1" diameter) with a handle. Dip the blower into the soapy liquid and then blow carefully through the ring making a string of bubbles.

58

Kim's game
Age 5–9 ✎ *indoors*

▶ *Various small objects, blindfold*
Place a number of objects on a table and place a cloth over them. The cloth is then removed or held up so that the children look at the objects one by one for twenty to thirty seconds (depending on age). They must then recount or write down all the objects they can remember.

Alternatively, allow all the children to look at the objects at the same time. The objects are placed on a tray and the cloth is removed for the prescribed time. The players then write down everything they remember and they score an extra point for including the tray.

Kim's smelling game
Age 5–9 **4⁺** ✎ *indoors*

▶ *Objects and items of food with a distinct smell, cloth for blindfolding*
Before the party prepare in advance a tray of little pots or saucers of various things with a distinct smell, such as orange slices, soap, peanut-butter, tea-leaves. Make the contents of the pots appropriate for the ages of the children. Don't make it too difficult for the youngest.

The children are blindfolded and one by one they go to the tray and smell the pots. Let the younger children say immediately what they think they smell. Older children can write down what they think they have smelled afterwards.

Kim's tasting game
Age 5–9 **4⁺** ✎ *indoors*

Before the party prepare plates of different little things to eat, such as pieces of chocolate, cake, carrot, cheese and so on. There should be one plate for each child. The children are blindfolded and sit at the table. Put a plate in front of each child. When you say 'start' the children eat the things and write down what they have tasted.

Kim's touching game
Age 5–9 **6⁺** ○ *indoors*

▶ *A number of small objects*
The children stand close together in a circle blindfolded with their hands behind their backs. Place an object in one of the children's hands. They feel the object then pass it on to the next child. Give the first child another object and continue in the same way until all the objects have been passed round and returned. The blindfolds are removed and the children write down what they think they have touched. If you are playing the game with older children you can have more objects and make them more difficult.

Pick up sticks
Age 5–9 **4-8** *indoors*

▶ *Cocktail sticks or spillikins*
Hold the spillikins upright in your hand on the table. Let go so that the spillikins fall higgledy-piggledy on top of each other. Each child takes it in turns to try to remove one spillikin after the other from the pile without moving any of the others. If they do dislodge any of the others it is the next player's turn. The player with the most spillikins at the end is the winner.

Collecting candies
Age 5–9 **3⁺** *indoors*

▶ *A dish with sweets (candies) in it, a blunt knife, a dice*
Place a dish of sweets in the middle of the table. The children take it in turns to throw a dice. The first to throw a six tries to remove a sweet from the dish using a blunt knife. At the same time the other children carry on throwing the dice until someone else throws a six. It is then their turn to try to extract a sweet.

Who, what and where?
Age 5–9 **3⁺** *indoors*

▶ *Three different coloured pieces of paper for each child, pencils*
Each child has three different coloured pieces of paper. They all write the name of a job or profession on one colour, an action on the second colour, and a place on the third.

The pieces of paper are then folded up, put in a basket and shuffled. Each child then takes it in turn to pick three pieces, one of each colour, and make a sentence out of them. This can be very amusing.

You can also go on to let the children try to piece the sentences together into a story.

Shapes
Age 5–9 ✎ *indoors*

One of the children draws a shape on a piece of paper. It might be a square, a circle or even the outline of a house. The other children take it in turns to add something to the shape to make it into something else, for example, they might make a cube from a square, a clock face from a circle.

Alternatively, everyone draws their own shape and develops it into as many different images as possible. The winner is the one who creates the most images.

Blind art
Age 7–10+ **4⁺** ♟ ✎ *indoors*

▶ *Pieces of cloth for blindfolds, various objects or utensils*
The children sit down back to back in pairs. One child in each pair is blindfolded and given a utensil or object. They do not say what the object is but they describe its shape. Their partner has to draw

something based on the description they hear. Afterwards the pairs exchange roles and a new object is given to the blindfolded player. When the drawings are all finished everyone looks at them. Are the objects recognizable?

How long?
Age 7–10+ **4⁺** *indoors*

This is a game which you can use to link activities and to calm down excited children and prepare them for concentrating. Tell everyone that there will be a period of silence lasting for example twenty seconds. The children then have to guess when the twenty seconds are up and call 'stop!' Anyone calling out 'stop' too soon is out. Anyone who calls out 'stop' at exactly the right moment scores a special point.

My spaghetti's all gone
Age 7–10+ **4⁺** *indoors*

▶ *Bowl, spaghetti, dice*
Everyone starts with ten dry sticks of spaghetti. They take it in turns to throw the dice and the first player to throw a six begins. They throw the dice again and if they throw a five they put five sticks of spaghetti into the bowl. If they throw a four, four sticks and so on. After two or three throws each player will have only a few sticks left but if, for example, a player who has two sticks left then throws a five, they must take five sticks back out of the bowl. The player to get rid of all their sticks first is the winner.

You must not say 'uhm'
Age 7–10+

As this game can only be played with one child at a time it is useful if a child has been left out of a game or has not paid a forfeit. Choose an object and ask the child to talk about it for one minute. During that time they must not say 'uh', 'ah' or 'um' and they are not allowed to say the word for the object.

Variation:
The leader asks the child a series of questions. They may not answer 'yes' or 'no.'

Creative activities

Who can make the longest snake?
Age 7–10+ indoors

▶ *Newspaper*
Each child has a sheet of newspaper which they tear up to make a strip. The child who makes the longest strip is the winner.

Making mummies
Age 7–10+ **6⁺** 👥 *indoors*

▶ *Toilet paper*
The children are put into pairs and each pair has a roll of toilet paper. On the word 'go' one child in each pair begins to wind the toilet paper round the other to make a mummy. The first to complete their mummy properly is the winner.

Charades
Age 7–10+ **9⁺** 👥 *indoors*

Divide the children into groups and give them five to ten minutes to prepare a charade. You might wish to give them a context, such as books or television programmes or films. Each group takes it in turns to mime their charade and the audience has to guess what it is. You can make a competition out of this by having a jury to judge the performances.

Charades with compound words
Age 7–10+ **4⁺** *indoors*

Two children go out at a time and think of a compound word such as 'church-tower.' When they come back into the room the first child acts the church while the second acts the tower. When the word has been guessed the next pair go out.

Chain charades
Age 7–10+ **8⁺** *indoors*

A minimum of three children go out of the room while the others think of an action such as beating a mat. The first player then comes back in and one of the children acts out beating a mat. Then the second player comes in and the first player gives an exaggerated performance of what they have seen. The last player to enter then has to guess what the first person acted.

Fashion show
Age 7–10+ **6⁺** 👥 *indoors*

▶ *Newspapers, scissors, sticky tape*
Divide the children into groups of two or three. They then have a quarter of an hour to make a paper dress out of newspaper. Then the fashion show begins. You could wait until the parents come to collect the children and they can join the jury who decide on the winning dress.

Band competition
Age 7–10+ **8⁺** 👥 *indoors*

▶ *All kinds of things for making music such as empty bottles, tins, spoons, rubber bands, combs, tissue paper, dishes, wine glasses, string.*
Divide the children into groups and give them half an hour to make instruments from the available materials and play something on them. If necessary you can give them more time.

This is a very creative game for musical and inventive children. It needs some preparation because you will have to assemble quite a lot of equipment beforehand. The following suggestions work well.

Bottles filled with varying amounts of water can be used to make chimes. Saucepans and lids can be used as drums. A simple bass can be made from a strong cardboard box, a long cane and a piece of string. Humming through a comb with a piece of tissue paper makes a very distinctive sound. Hollow bamboo canes can be tied together to make a Pan's flute. The hollowed-out branches of elder can also be made into flutes.

New words to an old song
Age 7–10+ **6⁺** ♦♦

Divide the children into groups and give them a quarter of an hour to compose new words to a well-known melody.

Serial story
Age 7–10+ **3⁺** *indoors*

▶ *Cards with miscellaneous pictures*
Cut out a number of cards either beforehand or with the children. Draw a picture of something on them or paste on a cutting from a magazine. Shuffle the cards and let the children each take one without the others seeing what it is. One child uses what is on their card to begin a story. Then they say 'Now you can go on,' to one of the other children. The second child continues the story from where it left off but it now has to be about their card.

Things to make

Threading beads
Age 3–6 indoors

▶ *Beads, water colours, paintbrushes, quick-drying varnish, strong thread, thick needles*
The children can use different sized beads to make necklaces. You can make beads beforehand using quick-drying clay that does not need baking. Form little balls from the clay and pierce with a thick needle or cocktail stick.

During the party the children can colour the beads and thread them to make a necklace. Spray the necklaces afterwards with quick-drying varnish so that they do not powder.

Sweet chain variation
Large raisins, dried fruit, soft sweets, sweets wrapped in paper, strong thread, needles

Make holes in the sweets so that the children can thread them to make necklaces as above. Remember that they will inevitably succumb to temptation so make sure that you have plenty of sweets in reserve.

Decorating cakes
Age 3–6 indoors

▶ *Gingerbread or ordinary cake, icing, sweets (candies), chocolates, nuts, paintbrushes, grease-proof paper, piping bag*

Recipe for icing:
25 g (1 oz) icing (caster) sugar
1–2 teaspoons lightly beaten egg-white

Stir the ingredients together in a cup, if necessary adding a little more caster sugar to make a stiffish paste. Cover the cup to prevent the icing from hardening. You can make brown icing by adding chocolate powder.

Give each child a sheet of grease-proof paper on which to decorate the cakes and put a bowl full of all kinds of sweets (candies) onto the table.

Nearly all cakes with a smooth top can be decorated. For small children you can buy or make little cupcakes beforehand. Older children who have the patience to decorate a cake quite intricately could use gingerbread.

The children can write messages or draw pictures on the cakes using icing squeezed through a piping bag. Icing can also be used as glue to stick sweets (candies) onto the cakes.

Painting
Age 3–6 indoors

▶ *Water colours, paintbrushes, paper*
Painting can be a peaceful activity which children really enjoy. They can choose what they are going to paint, though it might be something relating to a story they have heard or something they have seen at the party.

Salt dough figures
Age 5–9 indoors

▶ *Salt dough*
Ingredients for about eight figures
4 cups (500g) flour
4 cups (500g) salt
1¹/₃ cups (300ml) water
brush
water-colour varnish
thin wire
cocktail sticks

Working with salt dough requires some preparation. You will have to experiment beforehand and check the temperature and length of time required in the oven. If the heat is too high the dough will brown too quickly. Also an uneven thickness of dough can result in differences in the colour.

Mix the flour and salt together and add some water. Knead the mixture to a stiff mass which comes off your hands easily.

Sprinkle flour onto a sheet of grease-proof paper on a flat surface where the children can work with the dough. Encourage them to make interesting shapes.

Lay the figures on a baking tray and place it in the middle of the oven. Set the oven at 100–150°C (200–300°F) for the first half hour, then raise by approx 30°C (80°F) until browned.

Bread figures
Age 3–6 indoors

▶ *Dough for bread*
Before the party you will need to leave the dough in a cool place to rise. It needs about four hours.

Ingredients for eight figures:
500 g (1 lb) wheat flour
½ tablespoon yeast dissolved in 300 ml (10 fl oz) lukewarm milk
50 g (2 oz) hard butter
½ tablespoon salt
3 tablespoons sugar
½ tablespoon aniseed

Beforehand make a hollow in about 400 g (12 oz) flour and pour in the combined yeast and milk mixture. Stir to a thick paste. Cut the butter into thin slices and add these to the paste along with the salt and sugar. Allow the mixture to rise for about twenty minutes in a plastic bag. Sprinkle half of the remaining flour onto the paste and stir into a dough. Knead the dough on a worktop sprinkled with flour until it comes off your hands easily. Leave the dough to rise for about three hours in a cold place or refrigerator.

The children can make interesting shapes and figures with the dough. As they are doing this heat the oven to 225°C (450°F).

Brush the figures with a beaten egg and some milk. Bake them for 20 minutes on the middle rack of the oven.

Cards with moving figures
Age 5–9 indoors

▶ *Stiff card or plain postcards, sharp scissors, coloured crayons or chalks, brass paper fasteners (optional)*
The children can make the cards themselves, including the moving figures. First they draw a picture on their card. Explain that it is important to draw a boundary line, for instance a line dividing the sea from the shore. They cut a slit on this boundary line so that, for

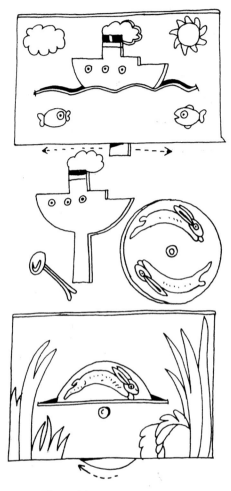

Figure 24

example, a duck can swim or a boat can sail. They do this by drawing the top of a boat and cutting it out leaving a long handle on the bottom so that the boat can move along the slit. There are many other possibilities, for instance they can make a slit along the branch of a tree and a squirrel can run along the branch.

Instead of cutting out figures older children can draw them along the edge of a circle of card. Have the circles of card ready beforehand. The circles must be smaller than the cards themselves. The slit in the card must be just big enough for the circle to slot into. Stick the circle through the slit and secure it with a brass headed pin. When the circle is turned different figures appear (see Figure 24). Warn the children that if they draw people they will appear on their backs or on their sides and disappear again on their tummies. Have a few examples ready beforehand.

Scratch art
Age 5–9 indoors

▶ *Plain postcards, wax crayons, cocktail sticks or thick needles, newspaper*

Lay newspaper on the table during this activity.

Give each child a plain postcard. They colour these all over with different coloured crayons. Next they cover the whole card with another layer of dark colour. They then scratch a picture onto the card using a cocktail stick or other sharp instrument. The top layer of colour comes away where they scratch and the colours below are revealed.

Painting pebbles
Age 5–9

▶ *Pebbles, water colours, brushes, quick-drying varnish*

Have ready some fairly large pebbles or let the children find them on a walk. After the walk the children paint the pebbles with water colours. They can incorporate the markings on the stones into faces. As soon as the stones are dry they can be painted or sprayed with quick-drying varnish.

Whirligig
Age 5–9

▶ *Pine cones, string, crêpe-paper 50 × 15 cm (20 in × 6 in)*

Make parallel cuts lengthwise about 1 cm (½ in) apart along the strip of crêpe paper. The cuts should extend to nearly the entire length of the strip of crêpe paper leaving a small area intact at one end. Roll this uncut end together and secure it with string, attaching the other end of the string onto a pine cone. Finally tie another piece of string to the pine cone (see Figure 25 below).

The children whirl the contraption round and round and then let go. The whirligig flies through the air and comes down to earth with the tail fluttering behind. Make sure that the children do not hit each other with their whirligigs.

Variation:

If you have no pine cones you can make little bags and fill them with sand.

Figure 25

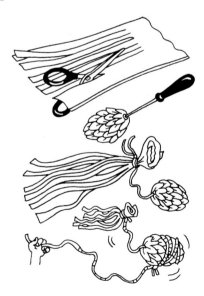

Spinning top

Age 5–9   indoors

▶ *Large beads, card, small cocktail sticks, coloured crayons*

Glue the cocktail sticks into the holes in the beads with the points of the sticks protruding a bit. Cut out a circle 5–6 cm (2 in) in diameter (depending on the size of the bead) from a piece of stiff card. The children colour in one side of the circle. Make a small hole exactly in the middle of the circle and stick the other end of the cocktail stick through it. The stick should fit tightly in the hole and the circle of card should then spin round on the stick (see Figure 26).

Figure 26

Dressing paper dolls

Age 7–9   indoors

▶ *Stiff white card, scissors, glue or glue stick, old newspaper and coloured paper*

This is an activity which you must prepare in advance. Draw a doll figure for each child on a piece of card and cut the figures out. If you wish you can copy and enlarge Figure 28. Give the dolls plenty of hair and let the children decide whether they are to be girls or boys and cut the hair to suit.

Let the children draw the faces and colour in the hair. They can then make outfits for their dolls. To do this they lay their doll on a piece of coloured paper or on an amusing printed pattern from a magazine, and draw the outline of the doll onto it. They then cut out the garment from the coloured or patterned paper leaving flaps (Figure 27), and then dress the doll.

Figure 27

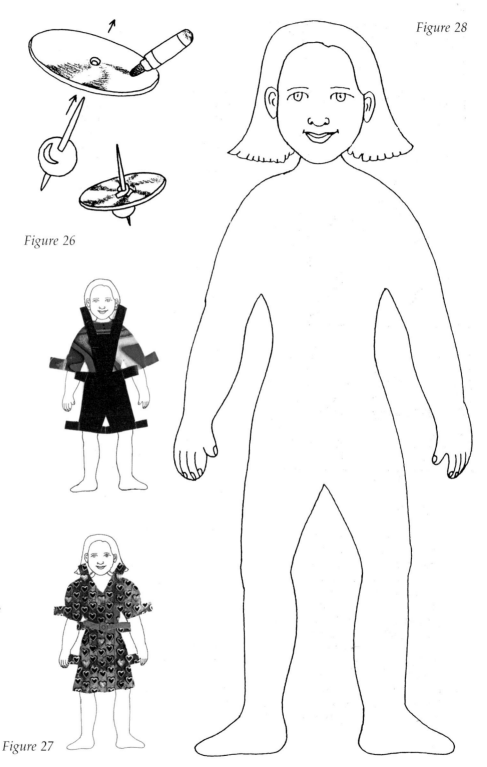

Figure 28

65

Figure 29

Potato printing
Age 5–9 indoors

▸ *Potatoes, kitchen knives, paper or cloths, water colours, paint roller*

- Cut the potatoes in half and let the children carve out a simple design on the flat surface using a kitchen knife.
- Next, cut about 1 cm (½ in) round the design so that it stands in relief. The children can then decide whether the design alone should remain or whether there should be an outside ring left as well, thus framing the design (Figure 29). Little children will need help cutting the potato and the design.
- Roll some paint onto a glass pane or a sheet of plastic. The children press the stamp onto the paint and then onto the paper or cloth. They can stamp one design on top of another printing with different colours, and so create a picture, for instance a flower. Alternatively they can create one group picture with each child doing a different design which together make up one big picture.

Making paper chains
Age 5–9 indoors

▸ *Coloured paper, glue, scissors*
See also Chapter 7, p.29.

Different shapes work particularly well for the concertina-style chain. You can think up all sorts of other forms in addition to the doll figure described in Chapter 7, for example, animal shapes. Make sure that you have plenty of examples on hand.

Making pictures on T-shirts
Age 5–10+ indoors

▸ *Plain white T-shirts, textile colours, safety-pins or elastic*
Take a piece of strong card the size of the T-shirt. Insert it into the T-shirt and pull the front tightly round it. Secure the material at the

back with a safety-pin or piece of elastic. The children can then paint a picture or design of their own choosing onto the T-shirt using textile colours.

They can also stamp patterns using a potato print.

Making masks
Age 7–10+ indoors

▸ *Stiff paper, pencils, coloured chalks or water colours, thin elastic*
The children make a domino or a mask which covers the whole face (Figure 30). Have a few examples ready for the children to copy. Alternatively you can draw a mask and have it photocopied so that the

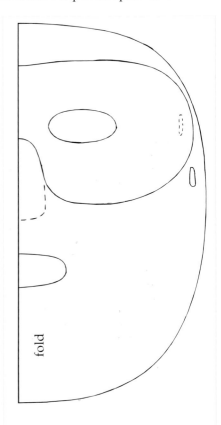

fold

Figure 30 (50% of true size)

children simply colour it in. The masks are then cut out and holes are cut out for the eyes to see through and for the nose to stick through. If necessary glue reinforcements to the place where the elastic will be fixed.

Button pictures
Age 7–10+ indoors

▶ *Coloured card, buttons, glue*
If you have enough old buttons the children can make pictures on cards by sticking on buttons in various shapes and patterns. When everyone has finished the works of art can be admired and perhaps given a title.

Simple kite
Age 7–10+

▶ *a long lath 80 cm (32 in) long, c. 15 mm (½ in) in diameter; a cross lath 60 cm (24 in) long, c. 15 mm (½ in) in diameter; a piece of wood 20 cm (8 in) long (to wind on the kite-line); glue; coloured kite paper; strong thin string, kite-line 100 m (300 ft)*
- Notch the ends of the two laths and tie them into a cross.
- Tie a thin string from corner to corner and pull taut (see Figure).
- Measure and mark the kite-paper to be cut out making sure it overlaps the frame by about 5 cm (2 in).
- Strengthen the corners by sticking on an extra bit of kite paper.
- Lay the wooden cross on the paper and fold the edges of the paper round the strings and stick it down.
- Turn the kite over and tie a string to each end of the long lath securing it at the notch. Do the same with the cross lath and

tie the middle of both strings so they are taught. The knot must lie exactly over the centre of the cross. When you lift the kite by the knot, the top of the kite will hang a bit higher than the tail.
- Make a tail four times the length of the kite itself. Tie little pieces of coloured paper along the tail at intervals of about 20 cm (8 in). Tie a bunch of coloured paper to the end of the tail.

- Both the kite line and the tail should be detachable so that they do not get all tangled up. Secure them to the kite with a toggle before you fly the kite.
- Finally tension the cross-lath below with the string to make a bow. This will give the kite stability in the air.

Fly your kite in open spaces and *never* fly it near electricity lines or in thundery weather.

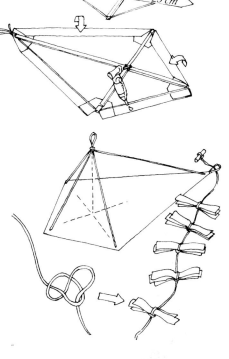

Active indoor games

Peas game
Age 3–6 **3⁺** *indoor*

▶ *Cups, peas, straws*
Everyone has two cups in front of them, an empty cup and one containing twenty peas. When you say 'Go!' the children try to suck the peas onto the straw one at a time, letting them drop into the other cup. The winner is the first to get all their peas into the other cup.

The seven year sleeper
Age 5–9 **5⁺** *indoors*

▶ *Large mat or lilo*
Mark out a circle about 5 m (16 feet) in diameter around the mat. The seven year sleeper lies on the mat inside the circle. The other children stand around the circle. The aim of the children round the circle is to tip the sleeper out of the mat or pull the mat from under them. The aim of the sleeper is to catch one of the children when they step inside the circle to catch hold of the mat. As the sleeper tries to catch someone the children on the other side have a chance to grab the mat.

Car racing
Age 5–6 **ᴹ** *indoors*

▶ *Thread, thin string, or stout woollen yarn, toy cars*
Tie strings to the cars. For younger children the length of the string should be about 5 m (16 feet), for older ones 7 m (23 feet). The aim is to wind up the string as fast as possible until the car reaches the winder. Younger children can wind the string round a card, older ones round their fingers.

Give me some clothes
Age 5–9 **8⁺** **ᴹ** *indoors*

Arrange the children into two teams and choose one child from each team. On the word 'Go!' each team tries to dress the chosen child in as many clothes as possible. They can only use clothes from children in their own team but they can use handkerchiefs as scarves. Stop the game after two minutes to see which child is wearing the most clothes.

The dark wood
Age 5–9 **7⁺** *indoors*

See p.42 for this blindfold game.

Hands on the table
Age 5–9 **6⁺** ♟ *indoors*

▶ *Two coins*

Divide the children into two teams, and seat the teams along either side of the table. Each team receives a coin. They pass the coin from hand to hand under the table but as soon as you say 'Hands on the table!' everyone puts their fists on the table. Each team then has to guess which member of the other team is holding the coin. If they guess correctly they score a point. Determine beforehand how many guesses each team is allowed. It is also a good idea to decide how many times the game is to be played or how many points have to be gained to win.

Winning the treasure
Age 5–9 **3⁺** *indoors*

▶ *A treasure, (for example a little present, or something nice to eat), cocktail sticks or spillikins, dice*

Build a wall of cocktail sticks round the treasure.

The children throw the dice. The first to throw a six begins. They throw the dice again and pick up and keep as many spillikins as the number shown on the dice. It is then the next child's turn. When all the spillikins have been removed everyone counts the ones they have taken. The child who has the most gets the treasure. Then a new treasure is 'hidden' inside the wall and the game begins again to give the other children a chance. If a child wins the treasure a second time they can choose who to give it to. The game can continue until everyone has won a treasure.

Up on the wall, into the ditch
Age 5–9 **5⁺**

▶ *An old bench*

This is a good game for getting the children moving. Everyone stands next to each other in a line opposite a bench which is the wall. If you do not have an old bench you can make the children go somewhere else for the wall.

When you say 'Up on the wall!' the children jump up onto the bench. When you say 'Into the ditch!' they crouch on the ground. Vary the speed and change the order of the commands, sometimes repeating the same command in succession to confuse the children. Anyone making a mistake is out.

Musical chairs
Age 5–9 **5⁺** ♪ *indoors*

▶ *Chairs*

Set out the chairs in the middle of the room either in a circle or back to back in a row. The number of chairs should be one less than the number of players. Everyone stands in a circle round the chairs. When the music starts they walk round the chairs. When the music stops everyone tries to sit down on a chair. One player fails and is out. Then the music starts again and one chair is removed. When the music stops again another player fails to find a seat and is out.

Variation without chairs

When the music stops everyone sits on the floor. The last one to sit down is out.

Variation with newspaper

Put sheets of newspaper on the floor instead of chairs. If necessary secure them with sticky tape. When the music stops each player has to stand on a newspaper, and each time one newspaper is removed.

Catch a balloon
Age 5–9 **5⁺** ♪ *indoors*

▶ *Balloons*

This game is a variation on *Musical chairs*. The number of balloons should be one less than the number of children. As soon as the music begins all the balloons are sent up into the air. When the music stops everyone tries to grab a balloon. The child who does not get one leaves the game. One balloon is then removed and the game starts again. Continue until there is only one child left.

69

Blowing the balloon
Age 7–9 **5⁺** ⚬

▸ *Balloons*

You will need plenty of space for this game. It can be played out of doors if there is not too much wind. The children stand in a circle holding hands. If there are more than eight children they hold hands alternately, behind or in front of their immediate neighbours, so that the circle becomes tighter. Stand outside the circle and toss a blown-up balloon up into the air above the children. The children try to keep the balloon in the air by blowing at it without letting go of each other's hands.

Who's got the longest string?
Age 5–9 **4⁺** *indoors*

▸ *String or yarn*

Cut the string or wool into several pieces of different lengths and hide them all around the room. The children look for the pieces of string and tie the ones they find together to make one long piece of string. The one with the longest piece of string wins.

Across the line
Age 7–10+ **2⁺**

▸ *Sticky tape or a piece of chalk*

Mark a dividing line along the floor or ground using a piece of sticky tape or some chalk. Two children stand back to back across the line. They bend down and stretch their hands backwards through their legs to take hold of each other's hands. When you say 'Pull!' they pull until one child manages to pull the other over the line. You can hold rounds so that winners of the first round enter the second round and so on until the final.

Mind your toes
Age 7–10+ **8⁺** ⚬ *indoors*

All the children except for one join hands in a circle. The extra child (or, if there are a lot of children, two extra children) stand in the middle. Everyone is barefoot. The child in the middle tries to step on the other children's toes. The children in the circle must not let go of each other's hands but they can side-step, jump away, or hop, to avoid getting trodden on. If the child in the middle succeeds in stepping on someone's toes that child then takes their place.

Blindfold games

Pin the tail on the donkey
Age 5–9 **4⁺** *indoors*

▸ *A large drawing of a donkey without a tail, the tail of the donkey made of stiff card, a thumb tack*

Draw a large donkey without a tail on a piece of card and hang it on the wall. The children are blindfolded in turn, given the tail with the thumb tack and led to a point about 4 m (12 feet) away from the donkey. Each child then moves towards the donkey and fixes the donkey's tail where they think it should be. Mark the spot each child chooses and write their name next to it. Once everyone has had a turn let them all have a look to see who chose the best place.

Hitting the tin
Age 5–9

▶ *An empty tin, a stick, something nice (perhaps a small cookie or cake)*
Place a tin anywhere on the floor or ground and put something nice in it. Blindfold one of the children and put a stick in their hand. Turn the child round two or three times. They have to try to hit the tin with the stick in a certain number of swipes. If they succeed they win whatever is in the tin.

Blindman's buff
Age 5–9 **5⁺**

One of the children is blindfolded and tries to catch one of the other children who are running around. If they succeed that child becomes the blindman. Make sure that the game is played in a clearly defined area with no obstacles for the blind-folded child to fall over. This might be played indoors but it could also be in a clearing in a wood with a rope running round the trees to contain the area for the game.

Variation:
The blindman must guess who they have caught by feeling them.

Imitating sounds
Age 5–9 **4⁺**

One of the children is blindfolded and is told to listen carefully. One after the other the other children make sounds such as scraping a foot, stamping, tapping a piece of wood. The blindfolded child then removes their blindfold and must try to re-enact the sounds in the correct order. The winner is the one who gets the most sounds in the correct order.

How many socks?
Age 5–9 **6⁺** *indoors*

▶ *Thick gloves and old socks, two cloths for blindfolds*
Two children put on thick gloves and are blindfolded. A heap of socks is placed between them. They have to put on as many socks as they can in the space of two or three minutes. The one with the most socks on is the winner. Then it is the next pair's turn.

Jacob, where are you?
Age 5–9 **6⁺**

▶ *Two cloths for blindfolds*
If you want to play this game indoors you will need a spacious room. If you want to play outside, you will need to enclose the playing area with a rope.

Two children are blindfolded and spun round two or three times in a corner. The first child calls out 'Jacob, where are you?' and the second child, Jacob, answers 'Here!' Jacob tries to escape while the first child tries to catch him. The first child keeps calling out 'Jacob, where are you?' and Jacob keeps answering.

Ring the bell
Age 5–9 **5⁺** *indoors*

▶ *A little bell, cloths for blindfolds*
All the children except one are blindfolded. The child without a blindfold rings a little bell every now and again, while moving around the room.

The other children try to catch the bell ringer and anyone who succeeds then takes over as the new bell ringer. If the children get too noisy you can give the bell ringer a very softly tinkling bell or something which makes only a gentle sound so that the other children have listen carefully.

Rat catcher
Age 5–9 **5⁺ O** *indoors*

▶ *A plastic or paper cup with a tight-fitting lid, peas or gravel, a cloth for a blindfold*
Put the peas in the cup and check that the lid fits tightly. The children stand in a wide circle with one child in the middle wearing a blindfold. The children in the circle throw the rattling cup to each other. Each time the catcher must hold the cup for five seconds before throwing it to someone else. Meanwhile the blindfolded player points to whoever they think has the 'rat.' If they are right the two players change roles.

Dress on six
Age 7–10+ **8⁺ O** *indoors*

▶ *Clothes, dice, blindfold*
The children sit in a circle and take turns to throw the dice. One child is blindfolded and they sit in the middle of the circle with a heap of clothes which they pick up one by one. When one of the players in the ring throws a six they quickly snatch a piece of clothing from the blindman's hand and try to get it on before the next six is thrown. If they do not succeed they must give the piece of clothing to that player. At the end of the game, when all the clothes are on the players, the children decide who looks the funniest.

Who touched you?
Age 5–9 **7⁺ O** *indoors*

▶ *Blindfold*
One player is blindfolded and stands in the middle of a circle. One of the children in the circle creeps up quietly and touches the blindfolded child, then goes straight back to their place. The blindfold is then removed and the child looks round the ring and tries to guess who touched them. Whoever it was may give the game away by giggling.

Say something
Age 5–9 **8⁺ O** *indoors*

▶ *Blindfold*
The children stand in a circle, except for one child who is blindfolded and spun round a few times inside the circle. The blindfolded child calls out 'Say something.' The player opposite must then say something, trying to disguise their voice. The blindfolded child then has three guesses to guess who it was. If they cannot guess they are spun round again and must try again. If they guess correctly, the two children change places.

What was that noise?
Age 5–9 ✎ *indoors*

▶ *Blindfold*
All the players are blindfolded. You then make a series of noises such as opening a window, turning a door handle, putting a cup down on a saucer, pouring out tea, crackling paper and so on. The blindfolds are then removed and each child writes down what the noises were in the correct order.

Blind writing
Age 7–10+ **4⁺** ✎ *indoors*

▶ *Blindfold*
One of the children is blindfolded and given a pencil and a piece of paper. Another child 'helps' them to write a word by guiding their hand. The blindfolded child does not know what the word is. When the word has been written they take the blindfold off, and try to guess what the word is. This is not easy and depends on whether they have the ability to imagine what they have written. Take care that children who cannot guess their word do not go on trying indefinitely.

The guardian of the treasure
Age 7–10+ **4⁺** *indoors*

▶ *Treasure, blindfold*
One child is chosen to be the guardian of the treasure. They sit blindfolded on a chair and have to guard the treasure under the chair. The other children make a circle around the guardian. One of them is the thief and has to try to steal the treasure. If the guardian hears the thief they call 'Stop thief!' Then the thief has to return to their place and the next child has a turn.

Depending on the ages of the children you can make it easier or harder for them to steal the treasure. For example, if you want to make it harder you can choose a treasure that makes a noise, like a dish of marbles or a bunch of keys.

When the whistle blows
Age 7–10+ **8⁺** ○ ◗

▶ *Whistle, ball, blindfold*
One child is blindfolded and is given a whistle. The other children stand in a circle round the blindfolded child. They pass the ball to each other as quickly as possible as whoever has the ball when the whistle blows is out. The last player left becomes the whistler in the next round.

The king has a headache
Age 7–10+ **5⁺** *indoors*

▶ *Chairs, blindfold*
Place three chairs in a line. One child is blindfolded. This child is the king and must sit on the middle chair. Explain that the king has a headache. One by one the other children try to go and sit on one of the chairs next to the king, as quietly as possible. As soon as the king hears anything he cries 'Oh my head!' Whoever it was who was trying to sit on the chair then has to go back to their place.

73

Games of skill

Bobbing for apples
Age 5–9

▶ *Basin or tub with water, an apple for each child, towels*

Float some apples in a basin or tub. With their hands behind their backs, the children take it in turns to try and get hold of an apple. The little ones may need some help.

Knocking down the pyramid
Age 5–10+

▶ *A plank of wood, two boxes, fifteen empty tins, three little balls*

Place a plank of wood on two pillars (boxes) at the children's shoulder height. Build a pyramid of tins on the plank, using five tins for the bottom row, four for the next row, then three, two and one. The children then stand behind a line 4–5 m (12–16 ft) away. Each child takes it in turns to throw three balls and tries to knock down as many tins as possible. After each shot the tins remaining on the plank are set up properly again. After the three shots, the number of fallen tins are counted and the child scores that number of points.

Hoop-la
Age 5–10+ **6⁺** *outdoors*

▶ *Sticks or bottles, five large rings or hoops (diameter 20 cm, 8 in), if necessary made from stiff cardboard.*

Stick an odd number of sticks (five, seven or nine) in the ground at irregular intervals. Draw a line about 2 m (6 feet) from the nearest stick. The children stand behind the line and take it in turns to try to throw the rings over the sticks. A ring over the nearest stick scores one point, over the next nearest two, and so on.

Indoor variation
Use bottles instead of sticks and place each one on a piece of paper marked with the number of points to be scored.

Out of the circle
Age 7–10+ **2⁺** 🏃 *outdoors*

▶ *Chalk*

Two children sit back to back on the ground. Draw a circle round them. On the word 'Go!' they try to push each other out of the circle keeping their bottoms on the ground. The winner can play again with another child.

Spin the plate
Age 7–10+ **5⁺** ○ *indoors*

▶ *Tin or plastic plate*
The children sit in a circle. One child comes into the middle, spins the plate and calls out the name of one of the other children. This child has to catch the plate before it falls. It is then their turn to spin the plate and call a name. If anyone fails to catch the plate before it falls they are out.

Three way pull
Age 7–10+ **6** or **9**

▶ *A piece of rope about 3 m (10 feet) long, three books*
Tie the ends of the rope together to make a ring. Place three children in a triangle, each holding the rope so that the slack is taken up. Place a book on the floor about a metre (3 feet) behind each child. On 'Ready, steady, go!' each child tries to pull backwards and pick up the book with one hand while still holding the rope with the other. As one player approaches their book the other two can team up against them, but usually everyone is too busy trying to get their own book. The winner of each trio can enter the second round. If necessary the final can be played between two players.

Catch and other outdoor games

Grandmother's footsteps
Age 5–9 **6⁺** *outdoors*

The child who has been chosen to be 'Grandmother' stands facing a wall or tree. The other children all stand behind a line about 10–15 m (30–50 feet) away. On the word 'Go' they begin to step quietly towards 'Grandmother.'

'Grandmother' can turn round whenever she wants and if she sees anyone moving that player must return to base and start again. When 'Grandmother' has turned her back again everyone takes a step, risks a run, or just stays still.

The first to reach and touch 'Grandmother' takes over her role.

Tree dens
Age 5–9 **5⁺** *outdoors*

This game needs to be played where there are trees. All the children except one chooses a tree for a den. When the game begins they try to run from den to den. The player without a den tries to get into one of the abandoned ones before it is reoccupied. The game can go on for as long as you or the children wish.

Bulldogs
Age 5–9 **5⁺** *outdoors*

Draw two parallel lines about 10 m (30 feet) apart. One child is the bulldog and stands in the space between the lines. The other players stand behind one (or both) of the lines and try to run across to the other without being caught. If the bulldog catches someone they become a bulldog too and must help catch the others.

The merchant and the thieves

Age 5–9 **5⁺** 👥 *outdoors*

▶ *Articles which can serve as wares*
One child is the merchant and the other children sit in a circle (diameter about 2 m, 6 feet) around the merchant. The merchant's wares (articles of clothing, a comb, a dish etc.) are spread around and they have to watch carefully to check that they are not stolen. The thieves go round the circle and try to distract the merchant's attention so that one of them can steal something. The merchant can prevent this by catching the thief. The thief is then out of the game. The merchant loses if his wares get stolen.

The three countries game

Age 5–9 **9⁺** 👥 *outdoors*

▶ *Sashes in three different colours*
Mark out a pitch about 15 × 15 m (50 × 50 ft) or larger if there are a lot of players. The players are divided into three teams and each team chooses a country. Each country has its den at the edge of the pitch. The players of each country are distinguished by the colour of their sashes, for example, red, blue and yellow. When the game starts red sashes try to catch blue ones, blue yellow, and yellow red. When someone is caught the catcher takes their captive to their den before they can go on chasing. While they are doing this they cannot be caught. The first country to capture all the players from the country they are chasing is the winner.

Ferryman may I cross?

Age 5–9 **10⁺** *outdoors*

Mark out a pitch with two parallel lines in the middle. The ferryman stands between these two lines. The children stand behind the lines and chant 'Ferryman, may I cross?'

The ferryman answers, 'Yes.'

Then the children ask 'How?'

The ferryman demonstrates how, for example hopping, crawling, limping. The players then try to cross the lines as they have been shown while the ferryman tries to catch as many as possible, moving in the same way. When he has caught a good number someone else is chosen as ferryman.

Catch

Age 5–9 **5⁺** *outdoors*

One child is 'it' and tries to catch another. If they succeed the other child immediately becomes 'it.' You may have to determine boundaries the children must stay within.

Shadow catch
In this game the catcher does not touch another child. Instead they try to step on a child's shadow. If they succeed they call out the name and that child becomes 'it.'

Cross catch
While the catcher is chasing someone a third child tries to run between them. If the third child succeeds in doing this the catcher must stop pursuing whoever they were originally chasing and chase the third child instead.

Island catch
If the pitch is big enough you can mark out islands. A child standing on an island cannot be caught. This is especially good for little children.

Freeze catch
A child who is caught has to stay on the spot where they were caught. They then try to catch other children who try to get as near as they can to the captured children without being caught.

Catch and rescue
One child is the catcher and another is the rescuer. When the catcher catches someone that child is turned to stone and has to stand perfectly still. They can be rescued by being touched by the rescuer. Set the bounds of the pitch before.

Ball catch
This game can be combined with any of the above games of catch but instead of catching another child the catcher has to throw the ball so that it lands on them. Mark off the pitch beforehand otherwise the children can run too far away or hide so that the ball misses them.

Labyrinth
This game requires some preparation. Beforehand trace out a labyrinth of lanes with crossings and smaller lanes branching off. The children must stay in the lanes, without stepping over them or passing each other. The catcher tries to catch someone, but they too must also keep to the lanes. The others try to avoid the catcher by using the branch lanes. Anyone caught is out.

Feet off the ground
In this game you cannot be caught while you have both feet off the ground.

Head and tail
Age 5–9 **8⁺** *outdoors*

You will need plenty of space for this game. A school playground would be ideal. The children link hands to make a chain. The head of the chain must then try to catch the tail. The tail tries to avoid being caught and so pulls the chain away, but the chain must not break. When the head does finally manage to catch the tail the two children who have been the head and the tail now go to the middle of the chain and a new head and tail continue the game.

Over the line
Age 7–10+ **8⁺** **ᛁᛁ** *outdoors*

Draw a line on the ground. Two equal teams line up with all the children facing each other across the line.

On the word 'Go' everyone tries to pull their opposite number over the line. Once a child has been pulled right over the line they are out. The team which pulls the most players over is the winner.

Team tug
Age 7–10+ **6⁺** **ᛁᛁ** *outdoors*

▶ *Rope*

Draw a line on the ground and divide the players into two teams. The teams line up in columns on either side of the line and everyone takes hold of the rope. On the command 'Pull' both teams pull as hard as they can. The team that pulls the other team over the line is the winner.

Apples and pears
Age 7–10+ **9⁺** **ᛁᛁ**

You need an odd number of children for this game. Divide the children into two teams with one child left over. If you are playing indoors the teams stand along opposite walls. If you are playing the game outside draw parallel lines 6–10 m (20–30 feet) apart. The teams stand behind the lines. One child in each team takes the name of the same fruit, so that in each team there is one apple, one pear and so on.

The extra child is the shopkeeper and stands in the middle between the two teams. When the shopkeeper cries 'Apple' the two apples must change places while the shopkeeper tries to catch one of them. If they succeed they change places with the child they have caught.

Fishing net
Age 5–9 **8⁺** *outdoors*

Mark out a pitch and select three children to make a net by holding hands. They then try to catch the other children without letting go of each other's hands. Anyone caught in the net becomes part of the net until all the fishes have been caught.

Ball games

Who's got the ball?
Age 5–9 **4⁺** ◐ *outdoors*

One child goes and stands with their back to the others and then throws the ball backwards over their head to the other children. Whoever catches or gets hold of the ball stands with it behind their back. The other children also put their hands behind their backs pretending to hold the ball.

They all count to three and then the child who threw the ball now turns round and tries to guess who is really holding the ball behind their back. If they guess correctly they have another turn, but if not, the child with the ball takes their place and has a turn.

Foxes and rabbits
Age 5–9 **5⁺** ♦♦ ◐ *outdoors*

Divide the children into two teams: foxes and rabbits. Draw a circle about 5–8 m (15–25 feet) across. This circle is the rabbit's warren. The rabbits stand in their warren and the foxes are not allowed to enter it. The foxes have to throw the ball and get it to land on one or more of the rabbits. When they succeed they claim the rabbit the ball touched. You may wish to set a time limit before swapping the roles and starting again.

Stand still
Age 5–9 **4⁺** ◐ *outdoors*

One child has the ball, stands in the middle of the others and calls, 'Stand still. This ball is for John' (or whoever), and throws the ball up into the air. John must then try to catch it or get hold of it as quickly as he can while the others all run away. If he catches the ball he calls 'Stand still. This ball is for Hannah' (or whoever is named) and throws the ball into the air for her to catch.

As soon as the children hear 'Stand still,' they must stand still. When they hear a name they can run again. If the ball is not caught but lands on the ground the child whose name was called has to get hold of it and call 'Stand still.' Without moving from the spot they then throw the ball and try to hit one of the other children. If they manage then that child is 'ill.' If the same child is hit three times they are out.

Catch across the circle
Age 5–9 **6⁺** ○ ◐ *outdoors*

The children stand in a circle and throw the ball at random to each other. They can pretend to throw the ball to someone but then quickly pass it to someone else who may not be expecting it. Anyone who fails to catch the ball is out.

Variation for older children:
If someone fails to catch the ball they must squat down. If they fail a again they have to sit, and so on.

Rondo
Age 7–10+ **5⁺ O Ⓝ** *outdoors*

The children stand in a circle with one child in the middle. The others throw the ball to each other over the child in the middle, who tries to intercept the ball. If they succeed they change place with the thrower.

This game can also be played with groups of three people. Each group stands in a line and the two children at either end throw the ball to each other while the child in the middle tries to intercept it.

Line ball
Age 7–10+ **6-12 ♛ Ⓝ** *outdoors*

▶ *Rope*
This is a simplified version of volleyball. Set up a rope across the room or playing area roughly the height of the children's waists. Mark out a pitch on each side of the rope of at least 4 × 4 m (13 × 13 feet). The aim is to land the ball on the ground in the opponents' court, but passing it *over* the rope.

Knock down the tower
Age 7–10+ **6⁺ Ⓝ** *outdoors*

▶ *Eight or more tins*
Two children build a tower with the tins. They now defend it against the others who are the attackers. The attackers stand in a wide circle round the tower and bombard it with the ball. The defenders defend the tower by trying to catch the ball. If the tower is only partially destroyed by the ball the defenders are allowed to build it up again. If an attacker succeeds in destroying the tower completely then they become the defender and can choose their partner.

Catch the animal
Age 7–10+ **6⁺ Ⓝ** *outdoors*

The catcher runs about bouncing a ball within a marked off area. The other children are animals and the catcher has to try to hit one of the 'animals' with the ball. Each animal that is hit joins the catcher in trying to hit the other animals. Once there is more than one catcher they may not run with the ball any more. Instead they pass the ball to each other. The game ends when all the animals have been hit.

Sitting ball
Age 7–10+ **10⁺ ♛ Ⓝ** *outdoors*

Mark out a pitch 10 × 14 m (30 × 45 feet) and divide the children into two teams. Mark out goals at each end. The aim of course is to score goals but the children can only move on their bottoms and must throw the ball rather than rolling it or moving with it.

Hit and out
Age 10+ **10⁺ ♛ Ⓝ** *outdoors*

Mark out a 10 × 12 m (30 × 40 feet) area and divide it into two courts. The children are divided into two teams, one in each court. The aim is to throw the ball and hit one of the members of the opposing team. A back-stop from the opposing team stands behind each court and if they catch the ball they pass it back to one of their own team. A player is knocked out if the ball touches any part of their body, and have to stand behind the opposing team's court with the back-stop from their own team. But if someone catches the ball they win back a knocked-out player from their own side, who can come back onto the team. When all the players of one side have been knocked out they have lost.

Relay races

Relay races are always played in teams. They work fine with two teams but if there are a lot of children you can have three teams. In some relays you need the same number of children in each team.

Usually the first team to finish is the winner. The members of the team have to carry out a task one after the other. As soon as each member finishes they return to base and the next member sets forth.

Organize the relay to suit the ages of the children. It is useful to have an assistant so that you can both watch the teams.

Tin race
Age 5–9 **6⁺** *outdoors*

▶ *Empty tins*
Pierce two holes opposite each other in the sides just above the bottom of each tin. Take a long piece of string and pass each end through each hole and tie a knot at each end so that the ends cannot slip back through the holes. The children who are about to run then stand on a tin and hold the loop of string attached to it. The children need to decide on the exact rules for the race. They could either have each foot on a separate tin, or have both feet on the same tin so that they have to jump along.

Master and servant
Age 5–9 **8⁺**

▶ *Card, scissors*
You need an even number of players for this. Cut out two large pairs of shoes (simple shapes on flat card will do), one for each team. Each team divides itself into

pairs, with a master and a servant in each pair. When the race starts the first pair from each team sets off. The servant has to lay the shoes in front of the master for him to step on. When the master is standing with one foot on one shoe the servant picks up the shoe behind and lays it in front for the next step. The idea is not only to move the shoes as quickly as possible but also at exactly the right distance. If the master puts a foot even slightly over the edge of the shoe he and his servant have to start again.

Egg and spoon race
Age 5–9 **6⁺** *outdoors*

▶ *Wooden spoons, hard-boiled eggs (or potatoes)*
Do not give young children spoons which are too shallow as otherwise they will lose their eggs too easily.

Each team has a wooden spoon and a hard-boiled egg. The team members take it in turns to run with their egg balanced on the spoon. When they have reached the turning point they put the egg in their hand and run back to the next player in their team. If they drop their egg while it is meant to be balanced on the spoon they must go back to the beginning and start again.

Variations:
You can invent all kinds of variations on this game, for example the children could move in a specific way (backwards, on their knees, etc). You can also substitute the egg and spoon with for instance a glass full of water on a tray, a ball balanced on a bottle, a marble on two sticks, and so on.

Tunnel race
Age 5–9 **8⁺** *outdoors*

The children line up in two teams each in a single column behind a starting line. Everyone bends down to touch the ground with their hands so forming a tunnel. Call out 'Ready, steady, go' and the child at the back of each column crawls through the tunnel. The second last follows and then the next, and so on. When the players reach the front they remain there forming part of the tunnel. The team which has all crawled through first wins.

Footstep race
Age 5–9 **6⁺** *outdoors*

▶ *Coloured card, scissors*
Using different coloured card for each team, cut out an equal number of footsteps for each team. Lay the footsteps in a trail. Each child must run along their team's footsteps. Anyone who puts a foot wrong must go back to the step before. The trails can be made more difficult by intertwining them or by increasing the interval between each footstep.

Seven-league boots variation
Cut out a pair of giant shoes from card for each team. Before starting the relay mark the point at which the children have to turn round. The first player from each team begins by laying down one of the shoes and stepping onto it. Then they lay the other shoe in front and step onto that. They pick up the first shoe and put it in front again, and so on. When they get to the turning point they pick up both shoes, run back to the start and give the shoes to number two.

Three ball race
Age 7–10+ **6⁺** *outdoors*

▶ *Six large balls*
Each team has three large balls. On the word 'Go' the first child in each team runs along to the turning point and back, rolling the three balls along with them as they run. It is then the next player's turn.

Sack race
Age 5–9 **6⁺** *outdoors*

▶ *Sacks*
The first child in each team steps into a sack and pulls it up to their hips. They run, jump or hop along to the finishing line in the sacks. At the finishing line they step out of the sacks and run back to the next runner in their team, carrying the sacks.

Ankle race
Age 7–10+ **6⁺** *outdoors*

On the word 'Go' the first child in each team takes hold of their own ankles and runs like that to the turning point (5–8 m, 15–25 feet away). They then let go and run back to the starting line. The next child then sets off in the same way.

Three-legged relay race
Age 7–10+ **8⁺** *outdoors*

▶ *Strips of cloth*
The children form pairs within each team, and each pair is tied together ankle to ankle. Each pair then runs to the turning point (at least 5 m, 15 feet away) and back in relay. It is then the next pair's turn.

Blindfold relay
Age 7–10+ **8⁺** *outdoors*

▶ *Blindfolds, obstacles*

Lay out two courses with various obstacles such as chairs or boxes. The first child in each team stands at the far end of the course. The second child is blindfolded and sets off along the course. The first child gives the second child instructions to help them avoid the obstacles. If they crash into something they must start again, but if they reach the end of the course without any accidents they then guide the next team member, who must then wear a blindfold.

Creeping caterpillars
Age 7–10+ **8⁺**

The first child in each team kneels down behind the starting line. The next child kneels down behind and grasps the first child's ankles, and so on until the whole team forms a caterpillar. On the word 'Go' the caterpillars start to creep forward towards the finishing post some 50 m (150 feet) away. The caterpillar must not disintegrate on the way and must still be intact when it reaches the finishing post.

Dressing up race
Age 7–10+ **6⁺**

▶ *Two large jackets, two hats and possibly two pairs of large shoes*

On the word 'Go' the first child in each team has to put on the jacket, hat and shoes and run to the turning point and back. Then they quickly take off the clothes for the next child to put on.

Wheelbarrow race
Age 7–10+ **12⁺** *outdoors*

Each team is divided into pairs, a gardener and a wheelbarrow. The wheelbarrows walk on their hands with the gardeners holding their ankles. They move as quickly as they can like this to the turning point and back. It is then the next pair's turn.

Labyrinth relay
Age 7–10+ **6⁺**

▶ *Roll of toilet paper*

Roll out the toilet paper so that it stretches through the room or, if you are playing outside, over a flat stretch of ground to make a labyrinth. The children run along the paper to the winning post as quickly as possible. If they step off the track with one foot they have to go back two paces. If they step off the track with both feet they have to go back to the beginning.

Hopping relay
Age 7–10+ **6⁺** *outdoors*

The children hop to the turning point and hop or run back. Set the turning point at an appropriate distance suitable for the age of the children.

Pass the orange

Age 7–10+ **12⁺**

▶ *Two oranges*

The first pair of each team put an orange between their foreheads and keep it there as they run to the post and back. They must then pass the orange to the next pair without using their hands. If the next pair drops the orange they cannot go on until they manage to get it safely back between their heads.

Horse and rider

Age 10+ **8⁺** *outdoors*

Each team consists of one rider and a number of horses. The racecourse is 20–30 m (30–100 feet) long. On the word 'Go' the rider jumps onto one of the horses and the two of them travel as quickly as possible to the finishing post. There the rider jumps off, runs back to the start and jumps onto the next horse. The winning team is the one whose rider gets all their horses past the finishing post first.

Baton relays

Hair ribbon relay

Age 5–9 **8⁺**

▶ *Hair ribbons*

This race is for boys as well as girls. The first player in each team ties a hair ribbon in a bow round the head of the second player. Then the first child bows graciously and turns round again. The second player then undoes the bow, turns round and ties the ribbon round the head of the third player before bowing graciously, and so on.

Matchbox relay

Age 5–9 **8⁺**

▶ *The sleeves of small (match)boxes*

The children in each team stand next to each other in a row. The first child in each team passes a matchbox lid to the next child without using their hands. The obvious way to do this is on the nose!

Paperclip relay

Age 5–9 **8⁺**

▶ *Paperclips*

Everyone has a paperclip. On the word 'Go' the first child in each team passes their paperclip to the second child who then has to attach it to their own clip before passing them both on to the third and so on.

83

Firemen

Age 5–9 **8⁺** *outdoors*

▶ *Four buckets or pots, two mugs*
The children in each team stand behind each other in a column. In front of each team there is a bucket full of water and behind each team there is an empty bucket. The first child in each team has a mug. On the word 'Go' they fill the mug from the bucket and pass it over their head to the second child who passes it over their head to the third, and so on down the line. The last child empties the mug into the bucket and passes the mug back up again for the next fill. On the command 'Stop' the game stops. The team which has managed to get the most water into the bucket which was empty is the winner.

Orange relay

Age 7–10+ **8⁺**

▶ *Oranges*
The first child in each team has an orange. On the word 'Go' they jam the orange between their cheek and shoulder and pass it in this position to the second child, who receives it in the same position. If anyone drops the orange then they have to pick it up and put it into position again.

Ball relay

Age 7–10+ **8⁺** *outdoors*

▶ *Two balls*
Each team stands in a line with their legs apart. The child at the back of the line rolls the ball under the legs to the front and runs to the front to catch the rolling ball. Then they stand at the front of the line and pass the ball back over their head to the next child until it reaches the new child at the back, who then repeats.

Relays with tasks

Coat and hat

Age 5–9 **8⁺**

▶ *Two coats and two hats, markers*
Some distance from each team is a big coat and a big hat on a marker. On 'Go' the first child from each team runs to the clothes, puts them on (buttoning up the coat) and runs back to their team, and passes them to the next player who has to put them on and run round the marker. The last player has to leave the coat and hat at the marker.

Tissue relay

Age 5–9 **6⁺** *indoors*

▶ *Paper tissues, straws, an empty
basket*

This needs an even number of
players. Everyone has a straw. On
the word 'Go' the first child in each
team runs across the room to where
a heap of unfolded paper tissues lie
beside a basket. The child picks up
a tissue by sucking through their
straw, runs back with it and gives it
to the next child who picks it up
with their straw. This child then
runs back with the tissue and lets it
fall into the basket before picking
up another tissue from the heap in
the same way, and so on.

Hanging up the washing

Age 5–9 **8⁺** *outdoors*

▶ *A washing line, pegs in a container,
two baskets and clothes*

Hang the washing line 5 m (15 feet)
away from the teams. Each team
has an equal number of pegs. In
front of the teams are baskets with
an equal number of clothes. On 'Go'
the first child runs to the basket,
takes out two pegs and an article of
clothing, runs to the washing line
and hangs it up. They then run
back to the basket, for the next
article of clothing to hang up. They
continue until all the washing hung
up. The next child then runs out,
collects all the washing into the
basket and pegs into the container.
The third child then hangs
everything up again. The fourth
takes it down again, and so on.

Paper relay

Age 5–9 **6⁺** *indoors*

▶ *Paper, mugs, spoons*

Divide the children into teams.
Place a spoon, four little pieces of
paper and slightly further away a
mug in front of the first player in
each team. On the word 'Go' these
children put one hand behind their
back and pick up the spoon with
the other. They then try to scoop up
one of the pieces of paper with the
spoon and put it in the mug. As
soon as they have got all four bits
of paper into the mug it is the next
child's turn to try. The first team to
finish is the winner.

Feed the baby

Age 7–10+ **8⁺**

▶ *Several baby feeding bottles filled
with water, milk or juice, two bibs,
and two babies' bonnets*

Place a chair with a bib and bonnet
and a feeding bottle filled with
water, milk or juice a short distance
in front of each team. On the word
'Go' the first child runs to the chair,

85

puts on the bonnet and bib and sucks all the water from the bottle so that it is empty. They then take off the bib and bonnet and run back to their place whereupon the next child runs out and repeats the procedure. Before the second child arrives at the chair you need to have replaced the old bottle with a fresh one.

Variation:

This game can be played in pairs so that one child feeds the other. You can use spoons and mushy food instead of bottles if you and the children prefer.

Passing on the message
Age 7–10+ **8⁺**

Whisper a word to the first child in each team. This child then secretly mimes the word to the second child, the second to the third and so on. The last child in the team then runs up to you and says what they think the word is. Points are awarded for speed and accuracy.

Eating and playing the recorder
Age 7–10+ **6⁺**

▶ *Cakes and recorders or penny whistles*
This game can be a real challenge. On the word 'Go' the first child in each team has to eat a cake and then play the first line of a tune. Then the second child eats a cake and plays the first line of another tune, and so on until everyone has eaten a cake and played a line. The first team to finish is the winner.

Horse shoes
Age 7–10+ **6⁺**

▶ *Cloth for blindfolding, four little plastic cups*
Each team chooses a helper. The first child in each team is blindfolded by the second. On the word 'Go' they cross the room to where their horse (a chair) stands. On the chair are four cups. Now they have to shoe their horse by putting the cups onto the bottoms of the legs of the chair. When they have done this they take off the blindfold, run back to their place and blindfold the next player. Meanwhile the helper removes the shoes from the legs of the chair and puts them back onto the seat.

Group games and scouting games

Rescue the thieves
Age 5–9 **12⁺** ♟ *outdoors*

▶ *Two sticks to indicate dens, bands in two colours*
The children are divided into two sides and each side has a den. The sides take turns to be thieves and catchers and the catchers try to catch the thieves. When someone catches a thief they bring them to the catchers' den. The thief who has been caught is watched over by one of the catchers. As more thieves are caught they form a line, holding hands, in the catchers' den. The thieves who are still free try to touch one of the thieves in the catchers' den. If they succeed then all the thieves in the den are set free.

Hares and hounds
Age 5–9 **8⁺** ♟ *outdoors*

The children are divided into two teams, hares and hounds, and the teams have to try to stick closely together. The hounds chase the hares and try to catch them. If a hound catches a hare then that hare is out. After a while change the teams round so that hares become hounds and vice versa.

Follow the trail
Age 7–10+ 12⁺ 👫 *outdoors*

▶ *Small markers for laying a trail*
The children are divided into two teams. One team chooses a den and tells you where it is. They set off towards their den and the other team is not allowed to see where they go. They leave a trail behind them, but it might be a false one. The trail can be made up of chalk marks on the ground, scraps of coloured cloth or twigs. After a certain amount of time the other team is allowed to chase the first team and try to catch them. If the first team reaches their den without being caught they have won.

Thieves in the wilderness
Age 7–10+ 10⁺ 👫 *outdoors*

Divide the children into two teams: a merchant with servants and a band of thieves. Mark off a pitch about 20 × 10 m (70 × 35 feet) to be the wilderness. The merchant travels through the wilderness with his servants who fend off the thieves. The thieves try to catch the merchant but they have to watch out for the servants who can catch them. Any thieves who get caught are out. If the merchant gets caught the game starts again with the children divided into new teams.

Hide and run
Age 5–9 5⁺ *outdoors*

Decide the boundaries of the game beforehand. One child turns to the wall or a tree and puts their hands in front of their eyes and counts slowly up to ten, while the others hide. Then the child shouts 'Ten' or 'Coming' and starts to look for the others. If they see anyone they shout the name of the child they have seen and run back to the den. If they get to the den first the child they have spotted is caught and has to stand in the den, but if the other child gets there first they can free anyone already in the den. The game goes on until all the children have been found and brought to the den. The first child who was caught becomes the seeker in the next round of the game.

Hide and wave variation
This game is best played in woods or hilly ground where the children can easily hide and then come out of their hiding places to wave.

As soon as the seeker sees someone they call out that child's name and the child has to go and stand in the den. While the seeker continues to search, another child who is hiding can creep out and wave to the prisoner but of course they run the risk of being seen. When the children in the den have spotted someone waving to them they try to run out of the den and hide again, but if the seeker sees them they all have to return to the den, including the child who was waving.

Live ludo

Age 7–10+ **9⁺** *outdoors*

▶ *String, tent pegs, little flags, a large dice and coloured ribbons for each team*

Divide the children into teams of three or four. This game should be played with a minimum of three teams of three, but can also be played with four teams of four or three. Make a large dice out of cardboard or foam and mark out a ludo board with string and tent pegs. Then mark out a route across the board with flags. In each team three children are the counters and one child throws the dice. The first team to throw a six starts and one counter steps onto the 'board.' Then the thrower throws again and the counter takes twice as many steps as the number thrown. When all the counters from one team are on the board they have an extra turn when their thrower throws a six. The thrower decides which member of the team moves. If a counter lands on a place occupied by a member of one of the other teams they displace that counter. The counter is sent back to base and has to wait for a six to be thrown before it can start again. The team to get all its counters home first is the winner.

Catch the tiger

Age 7–10+ **14⁺** *outdoors*

▶ *Rope or old cloths*

Make a number of tiger tails from rope or from old cloths tied together. Tie a knot in the end of each tail.

Draw two parallel lines 5 m (15 feet) apart. The catchers stand behind one line, the tigers behind the other. The tigers tie a tail onto their clothing. They then try to get past the line of catchers without losing their tails. Any tiger who loses their tail is dead, but if a tiger manages to touch one of the catcher's shoes with their hand that catcher is dead. The game is finished when everyone on one side is dead. Then the teams can change round.

Capturing the flag

Age 7–10+ **10⁺** ♟♟ *outdoors*

▶ *A flag, ribbons or wool in two colours*

There are two teams: attackers and defenders. Everyone wears a ribbon in their team's colour tied round their arm with a bow or slip knot so that it slides off when pulled by an opponent. The attackers try to capture the flag and the defenders try to prevent them. A player is 'out' if an opponent pulls off their ribbon, and they have to stand on one side. As the attackers remove more defenders from the game it becomes easier for them to capture the flag. If they succeed in capturing it they have won. If all the attackers are put out of the game the defenders have won. If you find that the game is going on too long with only a few players left you can blow the whistle and start again, the teams exchanging roles.

Crossing game

Age 7–10+ **10⁺** *outdoors*

▶ *Ribbons in two colours*

Mark out a square on the ground. The square might be about 10 × 10 m (30 × 30 feet), but you can make it larger or smaller depending on the number of players. Divide the children into two teams and give each child a ribbon in their team colour. Each team stands behind the square at opposite sides. One child from each team stands inside the square and tries to catch the children from the other team as they cross the square. If a child is caught he must help to catch the others. To avoid confusion, once a child has been caught they must remove their ribbon or replace it with a ribbon in the other team's colour.

Treasure hunts

note of how long it takes to go from one point to the next.

- Make sure that the task cards cannot be blown away or spoilt by rain in the hiding places.
- Hide the treasure where it can be seen by the children if they look carefully. The final marker pointing to the treasure can be small and hidden somewhere unexpected so that the children might go straight past it.

The treasure

- Chocolate pennies wrapped in gold foil are extremely suitable as treasure. You could even put them in a tin or in a specially made treasure box.
- Remember that the treasure needs to be something which can be shared out among all the children who take part in the hunt.
- Make sure that you have a few pennies in reserve.
- The treasure can only to be shared out once everyone has come back from the hunt.

Story

The starting point for a treasure hunt can be a traditional or newly invented story, or a fairy tale or saga. The story should always be told before the treasure hunt begins. For children of about seven years old you might be able to act the story in the puppet theatre. In long complicated treasure hunts the story can be the instructions for the tasks and for information about the route, or can contain clues needed later.

Preparation

- Choose a clearly defined area such as a park. The size of the area will determine the length of the treasure hunt; in a small park of say 150 × 50 m (500 × 150 feet) it might last five to ten minutes. If you want it to take longer you will need a bigger area or somewhere where there are plenty of chances to hide clues.
- Make a plan of the area in your notebook, taking note of everything there is. Make accurate numbered notes of the starting point and everywhere where the task cards and treasures will be hidden. Make a

Laying the trail

- On your plan mark out the route with a dotted line going from the starting point via the various clues to the treasure.
- From your plan and the tasks you are thinking of setting, you can estimate how long the treasure hunt will take. The children will cover the ground at a half run so will take less time.
- Number the clues beginning with number two. The children receive number one at the starting point.
- Make a list of questions and answers, one for each numbered clue. Then write a card with a task and the directions to the next clue for each point of the hunt.
- Mark the trail with twigs, strands of wool, sand or stones, or draw arrows on the ground. These markers will disappear after a few days, so will not create any litter. Make sure that later stages of the trail are not visible from the early stages, otherwise the children might miss out a bit of the route.
- If necessary ask someone to keep an eye on the signs to check that they do not disappear.

Questions and tasks

- When you are making up the questions and tasks take into account the age of the children. If they do not understand the question and have to struggle with the answer they will lose interest.
- Disguise the location of a clue in sentences such as 'When you have almost crossed the wooden bridge ...' The word 'almost' indicates that the hidden clue must be somewhere on the bridge itself.
- Try to pose the questions in ways which challenge the various abilities of the children. A clue such as 'From the east gate go 84 fence posts to the north and then 11/12ths of that distance to the south,' will need a mathematician rather than a fast runner to solve it.
- Simple questions might be something like 'Which animals live in this wood? How high is this tree? How old is the whole team put together? Where would you sleep if you were lost and came here?' Tasks could be: sing a song about this wood, or make a wreath from things you find in this wood.

- Difficult questions should only come in the last part of the treasure hunt when the children have nearly arrived at the treasure and there is a strong incentive. The last question can be a teaser. If there is plenty of time and the weather is good you can send older children off on a false trail, but do not let them follow two false trails in succession.
- Check that the instructions such as 'left' and 'right' are correct. Nothing is worse than sending the children off in the wrong direction because you have looked at your sketch upside down!

During the treasure hunt

- Take the children with you to the starting point and point out the boundaries of the area to them. This will prevent you having to send out a search party for a lost group.
- Tell the children to keep together. They must bring back all the task cards with them so that they leave no litter behind. A missing task card can score a penalty point.
- Tell the children exactly where you or your helper will be if they get stuck or if anything untoward happens. Keep an eye on the proceedings in case they start quarrelling or go completely the wrong way.
- If necessary ask someone to make sure that passers-by do not remove the treasure or the clues.

Very simple treasure hunt

Age 5–6 outdoors

The minimum age for a treasure hunt is five. Five to seven-year-olds will usually prefer to do the hunt in one group and they will need the direction of an adult. The trail should be simple and lead directly to the treasure.

Use a story or a puppet show as a springboard into the treasure hunt. The following story is an example:

- *Punch is longing to eat a pancake, but he hasn't got any eggs and he can't buy them: they are sold out everywhere. At last he meets a little man who will give him some eggs in exchange for some red wool ...*

Then Punch asks the children to help him find a ball of red wool. By chance he finds a letter with a message for the children.

- During the treasure hunt the children have to look for a ball of red wool. Lay the trail with strands of red wool. The actual hunt only needs to last a quarter of an hour. You can hang tasks such as 'Hop to the next strand!' on the woollen strands. When they find the ball of wool they take it to Punch and get some pancakes or something tasty in exchange.

Simple treasure hunt

Age 7–9 outdoors

You can give questions to answer or tasks to carry out to seven and eight-year-olds. They usually need to be in one big group, accompanied by an older person. Older children may prefer to do the treasure hunt in smaller groups so that there is a sense of competition.

Make up a story or adapt a familiar one for the hunt, for instance:

- *Great-grandfather was the captain of a big ship. He was chased by pirates and he left a set of instructions which lead to where he hid his treasure.*

In the story you can refer to materials which you use in the treasure hunt. For example mention that great-grandfather always had a feather in his hat. Tie paper feathers to twigs on the trail.

91

Indoor treasure hunt

Age 5–9 **4-6** *indoors*

An indoor treasure hunt can relate to the theme of the party. The area for the hunt will naturally be much smaller and the emphasis will be on carrying out the task. You can therefore set more extensive tasks or ones involving making things.

- Mark out the boundaries for the hunt and give it a definite structure to avoid your whole house being turned upside down.
- Hide the clues in a consistent way, for instance in little glass jars. The trail then goes from jar to jar, and the children know exactly what they are looking for. Begin with a clue directing the children to the first jar.

Possible tasks:
- Draw the outlines of lots of letters, all jumbled up. Among them are letters which make up a word. Give all the letters a number, and check that the letters of the word all have the same number. Give the children coloured crayons and tell them to colour all the letters with the same number in one colour (so for example, all letters numbered 1 are red, all letters numbered 2 are green, and so on). In this way the word will be revealed.
- Set various questions with one word answers. The initial letters of the answers make up one word.
- Draw and write the directions to the next task in a rebus puzzle.
- Draw and cut out a jigsaw puzzle which when reassembled reveals a clue on the back.

Treasure hunt in your locality

Age 7–10+ 👫 ✎ *outdoors*

▶ *Pencil and paper, street plan or map*
This will help the children improve their knowledge of their own local area, but it will require more preparation as you will have to study some local history, plan a route through the streets and think up some relevant questions. Have one or two groups depending on the number of children.

- The tasks for this kind of treasure hunt will demand more from the children. To answer a question such as 'Who is the mayor of this town?' they will have to go to the town hall and ask the town clerk. To find the answer to 'How old is the town hall?' they may have to look on a wall plaque in the town hall.

92

- The challenge in this kind of treasure hunt is finding the answers to the questions although it can still end with a hidden treasure or prize. The clue can then be found in the answers to the questions, for example the first letters of the answers could indicate the whereabouts of the treasure.

Variation:
This treasure hunt can be done on bicycles. Do not forget to indicate on the invitation that the children should come on their bicycles.

Treasure hunt for two groups
Age 7–10+ ⚇ *outdoors*

Give each group a specific but similar task. Younger children could have six to eight questions and older ones ten to twelve questions. Each group has its own route but the routes are of equal length. Two treasures are hidden in two places. Work out the first route and then mark in the second. Organize the groups before you leave and give each group a specific colour of cards to look for.

- The preparation will take longer with two groups. You will need two to three hours to think up the tasks, with at least one hour to set out the route, and several hours to work out the details and a good hour to place the task cards, clues and the treasure.
- Depending on the age of the children, choose a large park, a wood, or a number of quiet streets for the treasure hunt.

Variations:
- If you have only one route for both groups the second group must leave no sooner than ten minutes after the first.
- You can let the two groups end up on the same route shortly before the end. Then there is only one treasure and it can be exciting to see which group gets there first.

10 Puppet Shows

Why have a puppet show?

Don't be put off by the title of this chapter; it's not a matter of producing a flawless show but of letting the children enjoy themselves and enter into the images and world of a puppet show. You can buy puppets, but it is much nicer to make them yourself and check that they are appropriate for the show you would like to do. You may find that your ideas for the show change slightly as you make the puppets.

Figure 31. Simple standing puppet

In this chapter we show you how to make three kinds of puppets: a simple standing puppet from a cardboard spool, a simple marionette and a classic glove puppet.

You don't need to start with complicated puppets. With little children begin quite simply and develop the puppets as the years go by.

Puppet show for three to four-year-olds

Puppet shows with complicated puppets such as elaborate versions of Punch and Judy are not necessary for very young children. A simple puppet made from a cardboard spool is quite sufficient (see Figure 31).

At this age children love to see things which they know already and so recognize. You can play on this by acting out everyday events which are familiar to the children, such as:
• receiving a present
• preparing a birthday tea
• going shopping
• a special or unexpected visit
• being ill on your birthday
• playing hide and seek
• losing and finding something
• packing up and moving house

Puppet show for five to seven-year-olds

With these slightly older children you can use more developed puppets. They might be table puppets or even simple marionettes on a table. After the puppet show you can let the children play with the puppets, though they may still be too little to play with marionettes. The story can now be longer and more complex, a real story rather than a single event.

Suitable themes for five to seven-year-old children:
• a night with the gnomes
• a magic potion, a witch, a spell and a happy ending
• Blackie the dog has gone missing
• Santa's reindeer has trampled on the presents
• going for a walk and getting lost

The following fairy tales can be adapted for a puppet show:
• Cinderella
• Sleeping Beauty
• Hansel and Gretel
• Red Riding Hood
• Rumpelstilskin
• Goldilocks and the Three Bears

Puppet show for children over seven

Children over seven still enjoy puppet shows. If the party has a definite theme it is good to bring this into the puppet show. You can also introduce a treasure hunt with a puppet show (see *Treasure Hunts* p.89).

General hints

Theme and story

- You can make up the story or choose one from a book or a fairy tale. Keep it as simple as possible.
- Think out a simple story around the chosen theme with a definite conclusion. It might only last ten minutes, for instance:

It's Jack's birthday tomorrow and he wants to know what his present is. While his mother is busy cooking in the kitchen he goes into her bedroom to search in the chest of drawers, under the bed and behind the chair. Suddenly in comes his mother. She laughs and says she knows it is hard to wait so long, but she has an idea: he can come into the kitchen and help her. So the time passes and when Jack finally goes to bed he falls asleep right away.

Next morning the time has come. Everyone sings 'Happy birthday to you!' Afterwards he gets his present and luckily Mother has invited some other children to tea, which is exactly what should happen on a birthday.

Props

- Make a note of the various stage sets. In the above story it would be the living room, the parents' bedroom and Jack's bedroom.
- Write down what you need for each set.

Bedroom: a little box or tin for the bed with a cloth for a blanket and two empty matchboxes for the end and head of the bed, a block of wood for the chest of drawers and possibly some other pieces of furniture, either from a doll's house or made from blocks of wood.

Jack's bedroom: a box for a bed, possibly some furniture from a dolls' house or made from bits of wood, a little tin or bag for the present.

Preparation and rehearsal

- The thread of the story must be clear and simple with a definite end. The run-up to the end of the story must be longer than the end itself. After the crux the story moves quickly to the end.
- If you act out the story a few times beforehand you will be able to work out what needs altering and what props are still missing. Changing the set too much can have a bewildering effect.
- It is better to tell the story spontaneously but if you find that hard someone else can tell the story, referring to a book rather than just reading it aloud, while you work the puppets. If you are doing this you will need to rehearse the play with the storyteller beforehand.

Figure 32. Father

Figure 33. Daughter

95

- In the story about Jack you mention that his mother goes into the kitchen but you do not show the kitchen. Try not to have too much happening off-stage as there will be nothing for the children to see on stage.

Telling the story
- Tell the story calmly and quite slowly so that the children can follow. Vary the pitch of your voice to bring out the nuances of the story and speed up when it becomes exciting.
- With longer stories or fairy tales you can play some music or sing a song between scenes.
- While you are telling the story move or touch the puppet which is speaking. Keep puppets or animals which are not on stage out of sight by laying them on a table, a stool or your lap.

The performance
- The children come in and sit down in a half circle on chairs or cushions in front of a low table. Whoever is working the puppets sits behind the table. Prepare as much as possible beforehand so that the children have plenty to look at as they sit down. You can talk to the children as you get ready.
- Keep everything as simple as possible. A house or a room does not need to be fully furnished. A folded cloth can be a bed and bits of twigs can be chairs. Green and brown cloths are all that is needed to represent natural things such as grass, fields or woods and a blue cloth can be water. Little twigs, stalks, pine cones, acorns and such like can be added to create a more detailed effect.

- Make sure that you have room behind the stage to lay the puppets and other props. An apron with a lot of pockets can be very handy so that you have all the puppets and props within easy reach during the show.

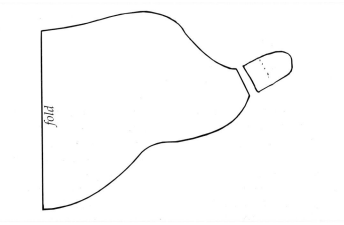

Figure 34. Smock for standing puppet

- Do everything very calmly and confidently so that the children feel that everything you do is part of the play, even if you occasionally have a look at the text.

Figure 35

Making puppets

Here are some simple instructions for making various puppets and a puppet theatre. If you want to do more sophisticated puppet shows you will need a book with instructions for making fully developed puppets and a proper puppet theatre.

Simple table puppets

▶ *A cardboard roll about 10 cm (4 in) inches high with a diameter of about 45 mm (1½ in) of cardboard, pipe cleaners, tubular gauze for the head, unspun wool or other stuffing, bits of cloth and/or felt, knitting wool for the hair.*

● Empty rolls of toilet paper or kitchen paper are very useful for making puppets. Alternatively, roll up a strip of cardboard and stick it together. Make a cut

Figure 36

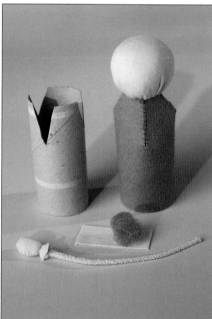

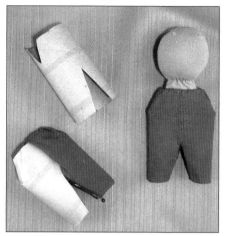

Figure 37

about 2 cm (1 in) into the roll and cut out a triangle out of the top, the middle and the two sides. Bend the sides and stick them together so that the roll tapers towards the front and sides (Figure 36).

● Clothe the cardboard roll by sewing or sticking a piece of felt or material round it. Felt is easy to cut and does not crumple. Leave a narrow strip of material sticking out at the top and sew the neck onto it (Figure 36).

● For the heads, roll a good tuft of unspun wool or cotton wool between your hands into a ball and lay it onto a square piece of tubular gauze about 16 × 16 cm (6 × 6 in) (Figure 38a). Wrap the gauze round the ball of wool and secure the piece round the neck (Figure 38b). Make sure that the part of the head which will be the face has as few creases as possible.

● To make a head without creases sew a second piece of tubular gauze tightly over the head. Cut into the top of this second piece and sew it tightly round the head (Figure 38c).

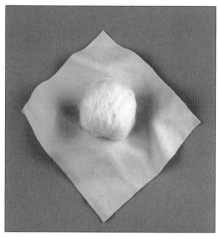

Figure 38a

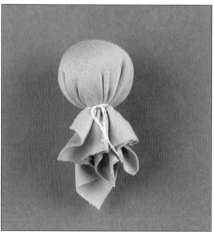

Figure 38b

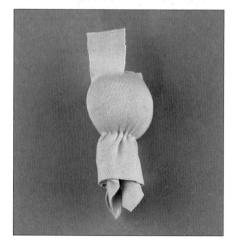

Figure 38c

97

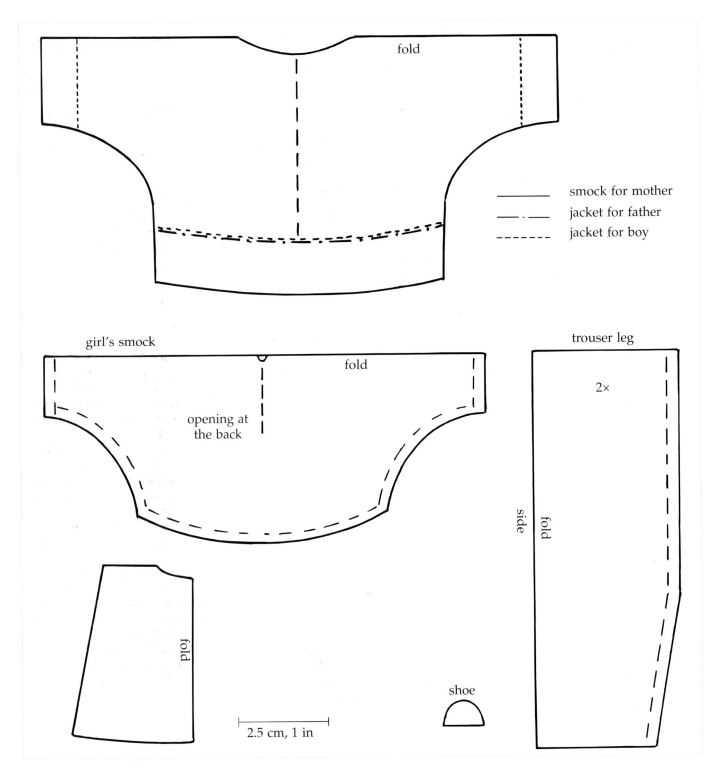

smock for mother

jacket for father

jacket for boy

girl's smock

fold

opening at
the back

trouser leg

2×

side

fold

fold

shoe

2.5 cm, 1 in

Figure 39

- Insert the neck of the head into the roll, first securing it to the border of the clothing with a few pins. Make sure that the head is set properly on the body before attaching the neck to the roll.
- Cut out a cardboard disc to cover the bottom of the roll and stick a piece of cloth of the same size onto it. Sew the bottom of the roll onto the disc.

Finishing off

- You can dress the puppets in all kinds of ways. Figure 39 has patterns for various clothes.
- If the clothes are made of fabric cut to the outside line to allow for a hem. If they are made of felt you can cut to the inside line.
- In Figure 37 you can see how the rolls at the bottom are made into

legs. The two loose trouser legs of Figure 39 cover the roll from neck to feet. Stick a little pebble into each leg so that the puppet will not fall over.
- You can make flexible strong arms and hands from a pipe cleaner. Curl the ends round and wrap a little unspun wool or wadding round them. Tie or sew a little piece of tubular gauze round the ends (Figure 36).
- Push the pipe cleaner into the puppet's smock or cape and secure it behind the neck.
- A simple hair-piece can be made by sewing a tuft of wool onto the head (Figure 32).
- Alternatively, embroider hair onto the puppet with a running stitch. Draw the hairline on the top of the head lightly with a

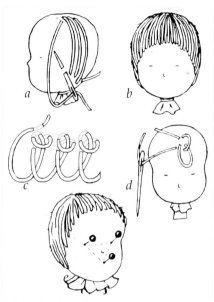

Figure 42

pencil. Stitch the hair from the top of the head downwards with long stitches. Leave spaces between the first stitches and fill these in the second time round (Figure 42a–b).
- A mop of hair can be made by stitching the whole head with loose loops. Sew them on one by one and then finally cut through the loops (Figure 42c–d).
- When the puppet is completely finished you can make the face. Decide where the eyes and mouth are to go by sticking three round-headed pins into the head. The eyes belong in the middle of the face even though they might appear at first to be a bit too low down. Stitch in the eyes and the mouth or draw them with a coloured crayon (Figure 42e).

Figure 40. Mother

Figure 41. Jack

Simple marionette

▶ *Tubular gauze, unspun wool, scraps of soft material, four little pebbles, wool for the hair, a thick thread, thin wooden canes*

- Make the head as described under *Simple table puppets*
- The body consists of the upper body with the arms and hands and two loose legs (Figure 43).
- Cut the upper body and arms from a piece of material folded double with the fold to the bottom. Sew up the top leaving an opening for the neck. Insert the neck of the head into the opening and secure this to the upper body.
- Make the hands by wrapping a piece of tubular gauze round a little pebble and tying it tight.
- Gather the ends of the sleeves together and insert the hands. Pull in the thread and secure the hands.
- Use oval stones for the feet. For the foot take a piece of material and sew it into a kind of bag in which the foot fits neatly.
- Cut out the legs from material folded double and sew up the side seams.
- To make trousers sew up the inner seams. Gather in the waist, turn the seam inwards and sew the trousers onto the upper body. Gather in the trouser legs, insert the feet, pull in the thread and secure the feet.
- The marionette's body is not stuffed so as to remain as flexible as possible.

Figure 43

Figure 44

Figure 45

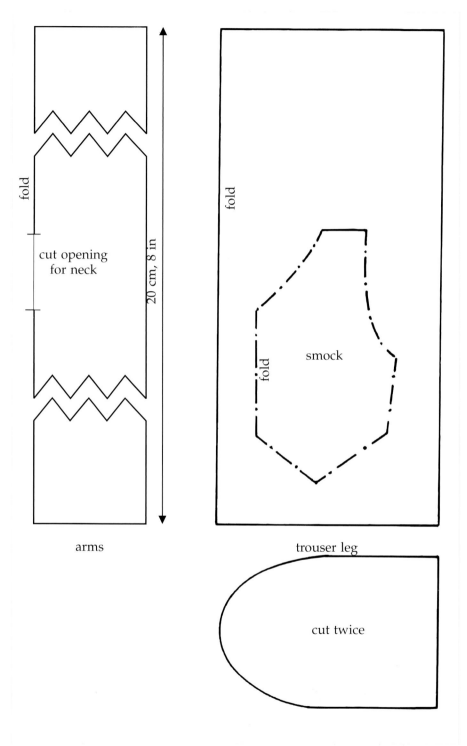

fold

cut opening
for neck

20 cm, 8 in

fold

fold

smock

arms

trouser leg

cut twice

Figure 46

shoe

The cross

- A simple marionette is attached to a wooden cross with three strings. One string runs from the back of the cross to the middle of the head. The string to the hands runs through an eye at the front of the cross. You can move them with your fingers (Figure 45). You can make the marionette walk by keeping it tilted up slightly and making it do little jumps.
- To move all the limbs independently is much more difficult and requires practice as your hand and fingers have to work too. If you want the marionette to walk properly the knees must be attached to the ends of the crosspiece, as in the giant (see p.18). The hands are attached at the front of the cross, as above.

Figure 47

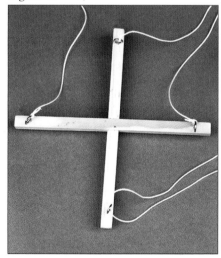

The classic theatre puppet

▶ *Thin card, papiermâché made from toilet paper, starch, pieces of material and felt*

Real theatre puppets have characteristic faces. They are easy to make from papiermâché. However you may be able to find clay which is specifically designed for making theatre puppets. Otherwise, 100 ml (3½ fl oz) starch is plenty for one head. Don't make more than two heads at a time.

- Tear the toilet paper into little pieces and keep adding it to the starch until it forms a flexible mass which you can mould. Pull the lumps of paper apart.
- Make a tube 6 × 2.5 cm (2¼ × 1 in) from thin card. Plaster the papiermâché round the tube and make a round head with a long handle for a neck. (Figure 49a–b).
- Mould the face but take care not to exaggerate the features. Note the jolly face of Punch and the sour face of his wife Judy (Figure 49c–d).
- Allow the head to dry out well. If necessary sand it smooth with fine sandpaper (see Punch's head in Figure 48).
- Paint the face.
- Cut out the hands according to the pattern and sew up the side seams.
- Cut out the frock, the collar and the cap from material folded double. Turn the material inside out, sew up the seams and hem the edges. Turn the right side out and sew the hands into the frock.
- Insert the head into the neck opening and secure the neck firmly to the frock. Stitch the collar once more through and gather it along the top. Sew the collar onto the frock. Sew on

Figure 48

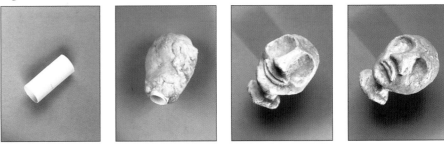

Figure 49 a–d

buttons if you wish and stick the cap onto the head.

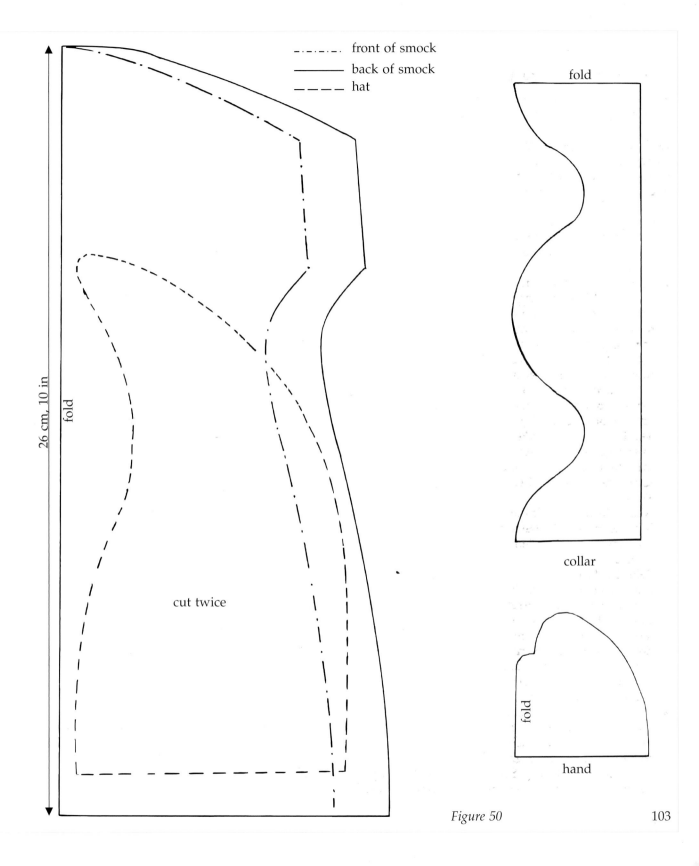

front of smock

back of smock

hat

26 cm, 10 in

fold

cut twice

fold

collar

fold

hand

Figure 50

103

Figure 51

Figure 52

Figure 53

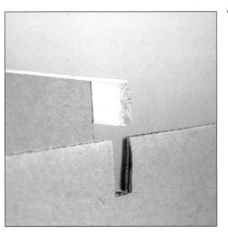

104

The puppet theatre

- A puppet theatre is a kind of stage. The spectators can see the puppets but not the people who are working them.
- A simple puppet theatre can be made in a doorway. Hang a cloth between the door posts. It should reach just above your head when you are sitting behind it. Hang a second cloth behind you for the scenery (Figure 51).
- Make a small puppet theatre with a front and two sides out of a large, strong cardboard box. Cut an opening in the front (Figure 52) for the stage and embellish the outside of the box. Figure 53 shows how to hang the backcloth by making cuts in the box. You can then stick curtains to the sides of the stage.
- You can make a temporary puppet theatre by removing the back of a bookcase or bottom of a drawer and hanging up a curtain as a backcloth. You will need a curtain rail if you want to have curtains which open and shut.
- You can paint a background for all the puppet theatres described above.
- You can make a proper wooden puppet theatre which will be ready for a puppet show whenever you need it. If you want to do this it is advisable to look in the local library or bookshop for a book with comprehensive instructions.

Alphabetical index

Alphabetical index of games and *themes* or *activities*

Index of Games by Type of Activity and Age

Type: ○ Circle; ♛ Team; ✎ Paper and pencil; ♪ Music; ● Ball

Numbering-off games

Page	Game	Age	Number	Type
39	One two, one two	3–4	4+	♛
39	Bands or badges	5–10+	4+	♛
40	One potato, two potato	5–9	5+	
40	Tic-tac	5–10+	2	♛
40	Connections	5–10+	4+	♛

Games for getting to know each other

Page	Game	Age	Number	Type
40	What does Johnny look like?	5–9		
40	How many beans?	5–9	5+	
41	May I introduce myself?	5–9	4-8	In ✎
41	Remembering names	5–9		○
41	Whose is this balloon?	5–9	5+	In ♪
41	Forfeits as a game for getting to know each other	7–10+	4+	In
41	Newspaper game, The	7–10+	5+	○
41	Who am I?	7–10+	4+	
41	Who will stand next to me?	7–10+	8+	○
	See also:			
40	Connections	5–10+	4+	♛

Games for linking activities

Page	Game	Age	Number	Type
42	How many balls in the bucket?	5–9	3+	
42	Pick the raisin	5–9	3-8	In
42	Dark wood, The	5–9	7+	In
42	How many names?	7–9	3+	In ✎
42	Tongue-twisters	5–9		
	See also:			
40	How many beans?	5–9	5+	
60	How long?	7–10+	4+	In

Action songs and games

Page	Game	Age	Number	Type
43	Follow my leader	3–4	3+	♪
43	Mulberry bush, The	3–6	3+	○ ♪
44	Grand old Duke of York, The	3–6	4+	○ ♪
44	Can you plant your cabbages	3–6	4+	○ ♪
44	London Bridge is falling down	3–6	6+	○ ♪
45	Big ship sails, The	5–6	6+	♪
45	Gathering nuts in May	5–6	6+	♪
45	Wallflowers	3–6	5+	○ ♪
46	Oats and beans and barley	3–6	4+	○ ♪
46	Ring, a ring o' roses	3–4	3+	○ ♪
46	Ship sailed from China, A	5–9	4+	○ ♪

Simple group games

Page	Game	Age	Number	Type
47	Biting the cake	3–6		
47	Sardines	3–9	5+	
47	Bon appetit!	5–9	5+	In
47	Who has most squares?	5–6	2-6	In ✎
48	Balloons	5–9		
48	Straw football	5–9	6+	In ♛
48	Flying animals	5–9	3+	In
48	Telephone whispers	5–9	5+	In ○
48	Lucky dip	3–9		
49	Hot potato	5–9	6+	In ○ ♪
49	How many things go into a box?	5–9	3-8	In
49	Don't laugh	5–9	5+	In
49	Donkey's tails	5–9		
49	Paying forfeits	5–9	5+	In
50	Redeeming forfeits	5–9	5+	
50	Hunt the thimble	5–9	5+	In
50	Hot or cold	5–9	5+	In
50	Who sinks the ship?	5–9	3+	
50	Musical statues	7–9	4+	In ♪
50	Fishing	9–10+	5+	In

Circle games

Page	Game	Age	Number	Type
51	Farmer's in the den	3–6	7+	○ ♪
51	Round the village	5–6	6+	○ ♪
52	I sent a letter to my love	5–9	7+	○ ♪
52	Busy bees	5–9	7+	○

Type: ○ Circle; ♟ Team; ✎ Paper and pencil; ♪ Music; ◕ Ball

Active indoor games

Page	Game	Age	Number	Type
68	Peas game	3–6	3⁺	In
68	Seven year sleeper	5–9	5⁺	In
68	Car racing	5–6		In ♟
68	Give me some clothes	5–9	8⁺	In ♟
69	Hands on the table	5–9	6⁺	In ♟
69	Winning the treasure	5–9	3⁺	In
69	Up on the wall, into the ditch	5–9	5⁺	
69	Musical chairs	5–9	5⁺	In ♪
69	Catch a balloon	5–9	5⁺	In ♪
70	Blowing the balloon	7–9	5⁺	○
70	Who's got the longest string?	5–9	4⁺	In
70	Across the line	7–10+	2⁺	In
70	Mind your toes	7–10+	8⁺	In ○
	See also:			
42	Dark wood, The	5–9	7⁺	In

Blindfold games

Page	Game	Age	Number	Type
70	Pin the tail on the donkey	5–9	4⁺	In
71	Hitting the tin	5–9		
71	Blindman's buff	5–9	5⁺	
71	Imitating sounds	5–9	4⁺	
71	How many socks?	5–9	6⁺	In
71	Jacob, where are you?	5–9	6⁺	
71	Ring the bell	5–9	5⁺	In
72	Rat catcher	5–9	5⁺	○
72	Dress on six	7–10+	8⁺	In ○
72	Who touched you?	5–9	7⁺	In ○
72	Say something	5–9	8⁺	In ○
72	What was that noise?	5–9		In ✎
73	Blind writing	7–10+	4⁺	In ✎
73	Guardian of the treasure	7–10+	4⁺	In
73	When the whistle blows	7–10+	8⁺	○ ◕
73	King has a headache, The	7–10+	5⁺	In
	See also:			
42	Dark wood, The	5–9	7⁺	In
59	Kim's smelling game	5–9	4⁺	In ✎
59	Kim's tasting game	5–9	4⁺	In ✎
82	Blindfold relay	7–10+	8⁺	Out
86	Horse shoes	7–10+	6⁺	

Games of skill

Page	Game	Age	Number	Type
74	Bobbing for apples	5–9		
74	Knocking down the pyramid	5–10+		
74	Hoop-la	5–10+	6⁺	Out
74	Out of the circle	7–10+	2⁺	Out ♟
75	Spin the plate	7–10+	5⁺	In ○
75	Three way pull	7–10+	6 or 9	

Catch and other outdoor games

Page	Game	Age	Number	Type
75	Grandmother's footsteps	5–9	6⁺	Out
75	Tree dens	5–9	5⁺	Out
75	Bulldogs	5–9	5⁺	Out
76	Merchant and thieves	5–9	5⁺	Out ♟
76	Three countries game	5–9	9⁺	Out ♟
76	Ferryman may I cross?	5–9	10⁺	Out
76	Catch	5–9	5⁺	Out
76	Shadow catch	5–9	5⁺	Out
76	Cross catch	5–9	5⁺	Out
76	Island catch	5–6	5⁺	Out
76	Freeze catch	5–9	5⁺	Out
76	Catch and rescue	5–9	5⁺	Out
76	Ball catch	5–9	5⁺	Out ◕
76	Labyrinth	5–9	5⁺	Out
76	Feet off the ground	5–9	5⁺	Out
77	Head and tail	5–9	8⁺	Out
77	Over the line	7–10+	8⁺	Out ♟
77	Team tug	7–10+	6⁺	Out ♟
77	Apples and pears	7–10+	9⁺	♟
77	Fishing net	5–9	8⁺	Out
	See also:			
87	Thieves in the wilderness	7–10+	10⁺	Out ♟

Ball games

Page	Game	Age	Number	Type
78	Who's got the ball?	5–9	4⁺	Out ◕
78	Foxes and rabbits	5–9	5⁺	Out ♟ ◕
78	Stand still	5–9	4⁺	Out ◕
78	Catch across the circle	5–9	6⁺	Out ○ ◕
79	Rondo	7–10+	5⁺	Out ○ ◕
79	Line ball	7–10+	6-12	Out ♟ ◕
79	Knock down the tower	7–10+	6⁺	Out ◕
79	Catch the animal	7–10+	6⁺	Out ◕